GUIDE TO
BUYING
YOUR HOME

Real Estate
Education Company
a division of Dearborn Financial Publishing, Inc.

Acquisitions Editor: Christine E. Litavsky
Managing Editor: Jack Kiburz
Project Editor: Karen A. Christensen
Cover Design: ST & Associates
Interior Design: Lucy Jenkins

Library of Congress Cataloging-in-Publication Data

CENTURY 21® guide to buying your home / CENTURY 21®.
     p. cm.
   Includes index.
   ISBN 0-7931-1783-6 (pbk.)
   1. House buying—United States.   I. CENTURY 21® (Firm)
HD259.C46 1996   95-50804
643'.12—dc20   CIP

CONTENTS

Preface   iv

1. Deciding To Take the Plunge   1

2. Evaluating Your Lifestyle   13

3. Using a Buyer's (or a Seller's) Agent   21

4. Finding the Best Agent for You   33

5. Understanding How Much You Can Afford   41

6. Choosing the Right Type of House   55

7. Winning by Careful House-Hunting   67

8. Negotiating an Airtight Contract   85

9. Finding Financing for Your Future Home   99

10. Securing Quick and Painless Loan Approval   125

11. Preparing for a Hassle-Free Closing Day   135

12. Moving into Your New Home   147

13. Decreasing Your Tax Bite   155

14. Ownership Tips for Your New Castle   179

15. Investing in Real Estate for Profit   193

16. Using Today's Technology for House-Hunting   201

Glossary   206

Index   214

About the Author   219

PREFACE

Buying a home is the great American adventure.

If you are one of the millions pursuing this dream, you'll want to be armed with all the information available to ensure that you find the home that's *right for you*.

That's where *CENTURY 21® Guide to Buying Your Home* comes in. In fact, if knowledge is power, this may well be the most powerful tool ever developed for homebuyers.

Step-by-step, this information-packed book leads you through the process of picking the right real estate professional, selecting a community, judging a neighborhood, choosing and inspecting the right home, negotiating your purchase and qualifying for a loan. You'll even learn about making the move into your new home painless and about maintaining it—and taking full advantage of the many tax breaks Uncle Sam offers homeowners.

This book is packed with 50 money-saving tips collected from our top professionals, designed to help you stretch your homebuying dollars. To address lingering doubts or concerns, each chapter ends with answers to the questions most commonly asked by homebuyers like you.

This level of quality is what you can expect from the company that symbolizes home ownership—and whose brokers and associates in your community stand ready to help put these strategies into action.

All of us at CENTURY 21®—YOUR best source for homeowner information and services—wish you the very best in *your* great and rewarding househunting adventure and many years of happiness in your new home.

CHAPTER 1

Deciding To Take the Plunge

Parents and grandparents often have advice for first-time homebuyers, and it's likely to reflect the way things were when *they* were young.

Parents may have learned about real estate during the skyrocketing inflation of the 1970s. The idea in those days was to buy as much as you could, as quickly as you could, with as little of your own money as possible. Then, as promised on those early TV shows, you'd just sit back and watch your market value shoot up.

"When we bought this house, the broker said he'd be glad to give us what we paid for it a year later if we changed our minds. That's how sure he was about prices rising. And he was right."

Grandfather, on the other hand, who remembers the Great Depression when those people shiftless enough to have mortgage loans were losing their homes right and left, may recommend waiting until you've saved enough money to buy for cash.

And as for prices!

"Somebody must be trying to rook you. I only paid $6,000 for this house when I came back from the second world war."

And today?

Owning your own home is still the best way to start building an estate. But you've got to consider current conditions, not the very different ones that prevailed one or two generations ago.

Today it's difficult to say just what the real estate market is, because it varies so much from one part of the country to another- and from one year to another. It will help if you get a feeling for whether right now, in your area, it's a "sellers' market," with fewer homes for sale than there are people who want them, or a "buyers' market," with so much offered for sale that buyers can pick and choose—and negotiate on price more easily.

If your local market is down, you'll be able to pick and choose, maybe negotiate a really good purchase price. If, on the other hand, houses are in great demand and prices are going up (a "hot" market), you'll want to get in as quickly as possible. Don't wait to afford your dream home, but get in as soon as you can. Then you can start saving up for your dream, and when you find it, you'll have something to trade in on the deal. In other words, there are better and worse times to sell a house, but it's almost always a good time to buy. And if you already own a house you're going to sell, it won't matter much what sort of market it is. If you must sell your home for less than you'd like, remember that you'll probably buy from sellers who are also receiving less than *they'd* like. Or if you have to pay more than you expected, you may well sell the present home for more than you thought it would bring.

In other words, when you're buying and selling in the same market, what you may lose on one end you can make up on the other.

Tax Shelter

When you start comparing mortgage payments with your present rental, you'll have to consider income tax savings. Once you own a home, you will probably want to forget about taking the standard deduction, because it will pay you to itemize.

Remember that all your property taxes are completely   ✳
deductible, and so is your mortgage interest on both a first and second home (unless you're borrowing more than $1 million to buy them—a limit that probably doesn't bother most of us).

If your marginal tax rate (the tax charged on your top dollar of income) is, for example, 28 percent, and you pay 5 percent state income tax on top of that, your tax saving would amount to 33 percent of your property taxes and mortgage interest. If your monthly payment came to $1,000, it'd be the equivalent of paying $667 a month in rent. Uncle Sam (and your state) would be paying the other $333 for you, and you'd see the saving in the form of a much larger tax refund at the end of the year.

If you want to see the extra money sooner, you may want to file a new W-4 form to lower the amount withheld from your salary once you have a mortgage loan. An accountant can help with the figures, particularly for the self-employed who file quarterly withholding estimates.

In addition, once you itemize, your deductions will also include expenditures like your state income taxes and charitable contributions.

☞ **Money-$aving Tip #1** *Remember to take income tax savings into account when you compare mortgage payments with your current rent.*

Then some day when you sell—and of course this sounds like discussing the divorce before the wedding—two fine tax breaks are available to you, almost the only free lunch on Uncle Sam. If you replace one home with another, you may postpone tax on your capital gain indefinitely (see details in Chapter 13). And when you're age 55 or older, you have a chance to take up to $125,000 profit completely free of any federal capital gains tax ever.

Equity Growth

Then there's the chance for equity buildup–*equity* being defined as the money you'd walk away with if you sold your property and paid off the loans against it. According to statistics gathered by the Federal Reserve, home equity is the largest single source of net worth in this country. It accounts for almost half of the average household's assets.

Investing in your own home is the foundation of estate building. Even if your area hits a recessionary bump along the way, real estate in general at least keeps pace with the rate of inflation, and over the long run it does much better than that in increased value.

Besides this appreciation in value, equity buildup comes from your monthly mortgage payments. Part of each payment goes to reduce the debt, the money you still owe on the loan. This principal portion of each payment starts out small, because you owe interest on your whole mortgage loan. But as you whittle down the debt, more of each payment can go toward principal each month, building your equity. The process is called *amortization* of the debt.

Amortization acts as enforced savings. For many homeowners, equity in a home is their principal asset, and many older homeowners regard it as a nest egg for retirement. Reverse mortgages, newly available to seniors in recent years, even allow homeowners to tap that equity without moving out or making monthly repayments.

To Buy or Not To Buy

Your own home, however, should not be considered simply as an investment. Most buyers want the control that home ownership gives them over their own lives. When you own your own home you can plant tomatoes, play the piano at two AM, wash your car in the driveway, paint your kitchen ceiling bright red. Keep up your payments, and you're set for as long as you wish; nobody can refuse to renew your lease.

When Not To Buy

There was a time when you could be sure of making money if you were selling a house in only a year or two. These days it's not so simple. If you don't think you'll be in town any longer than that, you may want to continue renting. Or if your rent is very low on a place you really like but you still want to own real estate, you might want to hold on to it and buy a small rental property instead.

Perhaps you don't enjoy tasks like mowing a lawn or shoveling snow. But if you want the stability and financial advantages of home ownership, there's a way to have your cake and eat it. Look at condominiums, where you can have the convenience of apartment living and still own your own place. If you want the tax benefits of homeowning but prefer apartment living, buy a condo or cooperative.

Protecting Yourself

If you are likely to be moving on within a few years, it's important to house-hunt with resale value in mind. You want something that will appeal to the largest pool of buyers. Consider the least expensive house you can be comfortable in; that means more people will be able to afford it when you need to sell. Buy something with at least three bedrooms; if you don't need the extra one you can always just shut it off or use it for storage.

Don't, in that situation, buy anything unique. No matter how attractive an unusual house may be, you could look for a long time before finding a buyer who has your tastes.

☞ **Money-$aving Tip #2** *If you may have to resell soon, don't buy an unusual or expensive house.*

Are You Ready To Buy?

If you lack cash for a down payment, if you've had credit problems in the past, if your income isn't quite up to the mortgage payments you anticipate, don't give up hope. There are hundreds of financing plans out there these days, and real estate brokers are used to planning strategy for each individual situation. There are often ways to overcome the problem that seems insurmountable to you.

Planning for Your Purchase

Even if you're not yet ready to buy, you can seek help from several sources. There's no obligation if you walk into a real estate office in the area that interests you and ask for preliminary help.

You can also contact a credit bureau and pull a report on yourself. Many accounts contain errors, problems that really belong to someone with a similar name, for example. You'd have to clear things up before you received a mortgage loan, so you might as well check early. Some credit agencies charge a small fee; TRW will send you a free report if you call a local office or 1-800-682-7654.

In addition, though this one will involve a nominal fee, you could apply to a local lender for preapproval on a mortgage. If you meet the lender's qualifications, you'd be all set, with your loan depending only on the appraised value of the house you eventually want to buy. When you have a commitment for your loan, you become very popular with sellers, which may help when you're negotiating a purchase contract.

☞ **Money-$aving Tip #3** *For a free copy of your credit report, write to one of the following:*

TRW Complimentary Credit Report Request, P. O. Box 2350, Chatsworth, CA 91313; Equifax Information Service Center, P. O. Box 740241, Atlanta, GA 30374; or Trans Union Consumer Relations, P. O. Box 390, Springfield, PA 19064.

To prepare your finances for the purchase, build up your cash reserve. Even if you won't need it all for the down payment and closing costs, it helps to look as solid as possible when you apply for a loan. Give up a few luxuries while you're waiting.

Don't make any unnecessary credit purchases in the meantime. When your income is analyzed, present debts will reduce the amount of loan you'll be offered. Don't buy a car until you have the house loan finalized. Remember that recent credit card applications will show up on your report and may look suspicious to the mortgage underwriter.

Also suspicious is any recent infusion of cash into your savings or checking account. If someone is making you a gift towards your down payment, get the money into your own name as early as possible. Otherwise, lenders will wonder if you aren't really borrowing that down payment, letting yourself in for more debt than you can safely handle.

A veteran may want to send away for a certificate of entitlement, just in case he or she eventually wants a VA mortgage.

The more you know about houses in the neighborhoods you think you'll want, the better buying experience you'll have. Start visiting open houses even if you're not ready to buy. Educate yourself by reading real estate ads.

How *the Agent Can Help*

It will cost you nothing to walk into a nearby real estate office and ask for advice. Most agents will be happy to discuss your situation and give you a rough financial analysis, inform you about price ranges in the areas that interest you, suggest appropriate mortgage plans and advise on how much you can probably afford.

If you have a home to sell before you can buy the next one, you might be offered an on-the-spot estimate of what your present home could bring, based on easily tapped computer data about recent sales in your neighborhood.

☞ **Money-$aving Tip #4** *If you have a house to sell, an agent can furnish a free estimate of eventual sale price.*

An agent can tell you whether, at the moment, it's a buyers' or sellers' market in your town. Agents may have information about houses that are listed for sale on which the owner does not want a "for sale" sign.

If you don't know how to pull a credit report, most brokers can do it for you right then and there through a computer hookup.

An agent can give you maps of the area and data about items such as school systems and tax rates in nearby suburbs or towns.

If you are more comfortable in another language than in English, you may want to find a bilingual agent. When you first phone or walk into a real estate office, you can ask if someone is available to work with you in your first language. Or you may find advertisements by an agent who offers that specialty.

Psychologists often rate buying a home right up there with divorce, serious illness, loss of a loved one and other potentially disturbing life-cycle events. Real estate agents know how to guide you through the whole process as smoothly as possible.

All this is standard procedure in most real estate offices. You aren't obligated in any way, you have a chance to meet different agents, and you can get some real help in deciding whether it's time for you to be a homebuyer.

Commonly Asked Questions

Q. How much should we have on hand for a down payment before we start house-hunting?

A. That depends on mortgage plans available locally and on your total financial picture. Any good real estate broker can tell you at the first meeting.

Q. Should we buy now or save up more and look for our dream house?

A. Usually, and especially in a "hot" market, it's best to buy whatever you can afford. Then start saving up for your dream house. When you find it, you'll have something to trade in on the deal.

Q. What will we owe to the real estate broker?

A. That depends on whether you're using your own buyer's broker and on whether that broker asks for a retainer. Much more on that in a later chapter. Meanwhile, it should cost you nothing to have an initial consultation.

Q. Can we visit open houses if we're not ready to buy yet?

A. By all means. It's a great way to start learning what the market is like, and you'll be welcomed by the agent on the premises.

And now to see if you've been paying attention, a pop quiz. Are you ready?

QUIZ

True or false:

_____ 1. Mortgage interest is income-tax deductible even on a vacation home.

_____ 2. Most of your mortgage payment goes to reduce principal in the first few years.

_____ 3. To postpone tax when you replace one home with another, you must be aged 55 or older.

_____ 4. The term *equity* refers to the value of your home minus the debts out against it.

_____ 5. The term *amortization* describes the gradual paying-down of your mortgage debt.

_____   6. The more credit borrowing you do, the better you look to mortgage lenders.

_____   7. You can't buy a home unless you have some cash, good credit and sufficient dependable income.

_____   8. Obtaining a credit report on yourself will cost about $20.

_____   9. It is probably not worth buying a home if you'll be selling again within two years.

_____   10. If you walk into a real estate broker's office, you will owe only a small hourly fee for initial advice.

Answers:

1. T	2. F	3. F	4. T	5. T
6. F	7. F	8. F	9. T	10. F

CHAPTER 2

Evaluating Your Lifestyle

Location, price and your own lifestyle will determine where you buy your home.

Usually your financial situation sets limits on your choice of neighborhood. That's why a good real estate broker starts off by helping you analyze your financial situation, to give you an idea of which areas fit your budget.

If you are moving across town, you probably know what area suits your lifestyle best. Coming to a new community, however, requires research.

One good way to learn about a new community is to subscribe to its local newspaper. Read it carefully for a few weeks, and you'll begin to get a feeling for neighborhoods. Write to the chamber of commerce and ask for information.

What Matters the Most?

You can also make the house-hunting process easier for yourself by some advance consideration about just what sort of home you want.

Before you start looking, accept the fact that you will likely give up something you now consider important: the fancy kitchen, the large backyard, the sewing room. You'll fall in love with one special house and suddenly decide you can live without a powder room after all.

To prepare, look through home and garden magazines. Drive through neighborhoods. Note what you like and dislike about your friends' homes.

Make a List

Make a list about what matters most to you. After all, having an organized wish list will help you remember what is truly important to you in a home. A lovely stained glass window is compelling, but it doesn't replace the need for a garage or the comfort level you would achieve from a secluded street. A list will help you keep your eye on your housing goal. Rate items like proximity to work, shopping, transportation, parks, city center or countryside. Do you want the creativity (and the bargain price) of buying a fixer-upper, or is top condition important? Would you enjoy the bustle of a major commuter center or the tranquility of a dead-end street? Do you need a top school district, or might you need to sell, some day, to others who would find that an important factor?

☞ **Money-$aving Tip #5** *Even if the quality of a school district doesn't matter to you now, remember it might some day to another buyer.*

How important is the lot? Do you want low maintenance or plenty of room for gardening and children's play? Are there types of siding or windows you dislike?

Which are absolute musts: dining room, eat-in kitchen, extra bath, two-car garage, guest room, fireplace?

Analyzing the ratings, establish your own priorities: factors that are essential, those on which you will compromise if necessary, those that don't matter at all.

If you prefer to buy an apartment, you'll find a discussion of condominiums, cooperatives and townhouses in Chapter 6.

Old Versus New

With an older home (a "lived-in," "previously owned" home) you may well get more space for your money. Old houses are more likely to have odd nooks and crannies. To some house-hunters these represent a chance for creative furnishing and decorating; to others they represent wasted space.

With an older home you're more likely to find large trees, established landscaping, sidewalks, sometimes big lots. In some areas property taxes end up lower on older homes. An older home may be "closer in" with a more convenient location for you.

☞ **Money-$aving Tip #6** *Expect lower maintenance costs with a brand-new home.*

On the other hand, you can expect more maintenance costs than with a new home, and remodeling can be expensive. With a just-built home, you'll have brand-new appliances and state-of-the-art heating and cooling systems. You can expect low repair and maintenance costs.

Construction problems, however, may surface later. With some developments, it will take several years before land-scaping softens the raw look of new construction. Until individual owners begin to make exterior changes, houses in less-expensive tracts may give a cookie-cutter effect.

In the end, though, most buyers make their decisions simply on emotional grounds. They like the character of older homes and neighborhoods, or they prefer instead the clean slick feeling of new construction.

Even buying an apartment, you may want to consider the trade-offs of old versus new. A mansion that has been con-verted to condominiums may offer original woodwork, fire-places, high ceilings. One just built, however, will feature the latest in fixtures and appliances.

Plan Ahead

Remember to look ahead when you envision your dream home. You may be sure about what you want now, but think about the future as you begin your search. Unless you are willing to move every few years, try to anticipate some of the changes that lie in your future.

Your dream home may lie deep in the woods now, but in a few years you could find yourself with two toddlers and no playmates for them. You might yearn, then, for tract homes in a neighborhood full of potential babysitters.

If you're facing retirement, you may want just the gracious older home you've always dreamed of and can now afford. Remember, though, that it may not be long before you'll want a first-floor bedroom and bath. Buying a home that's all on one floor now could save you a forced move later.

Ideas about housing design can change also. The couple with little ones will be delighted with a family room open to the kitchen so that the tots can be supervised while the cooking's going on. But ten years later the parents will be longing for a family room with a soundproof door, preferably out in back of the garage.

If you have an infant, you sleep with your door open, and you want to stay within earshot. In a year or two, though, you will value a private, quiet bedroom. Check whether the master bedroom is separated from the others by a zone of closets, hall or baths. (The best floor plans incorporate such buffers for all bedrooms.)

☞ **Money-$aving Tip #7** *Moving can be costly, so don't buy just for today. Consider how your needs and wants may change in the years ahead.*

An engineer's inspection can help you judge condition and is particularly valuable with an older home, but you are the only one who can judge whether a floor plan fits your lifestyle.

How the Agent Can Help

The broker can estimate driving time to work, shopping and other locations that are important to you.

An agent can arrange school visits for you. These days most school systems are sensitive on the subject of security; if you want to inspect them yourself it helps to have the broker set up appointments.

Real estate brokers must, by the nature of their work, help you narrow your choices if you are ever to settle on one house. Rigorously regulated by human rights law, however, brokers hesitate to characterize neighborhoods or give you opinions on school systems. If any of their assumptions are based on the forbidden factors— race, color, religion, country of origin, age, disability, sex—they could face charges of illegal steering (using subtle means to ensure that you end up where they think you should)

Brokers can, however, furnish solid data, and a good agent will have it available: per-pupil expenditure in various school systems, number of graduates going on to four-year colleges and the like. You can also ask the broker to pinpoint on your map the location of churches, fitness centers, museums, swimming pools—whatever amenities are important to you.

Commonly Asked Questions

Q. *Can I expect a broker to have statistics on crime rates in various areas?*

A. Because there's always the danger of violating fair housing regulations, brokers hesitate to give you such information. You can always investigate for yourself by contacting local police.

Q. *How do I find the best school system?*

A. Again, brokers can be in trouble if they try to characterize school systems. Besides, "good" schools mean different things to different people. An average student might feel overpowered in a high-achievement district. For some children, a school that stresses sports and athletics may be best. Ask for statistics on various school systems and judge for yourself. Often it helps to visit schools; you want one where your investigation is welcomed.

With the needs of your own child in mind, ask about school librarians and libraries, foreign language and music classes in the elementary grades, physical education programs, remedial instruction or advanced placement courses in high schools.

Q. Is it a good idea to let the agent recommend which neighborhoods we look in?

A. That's a difficult question. In a city where thousands of homes are listed for sale, of course the broker's expertise will help you narrow your search to a manageable size. But the law requires the agent to show you anything you can afford and to expose you to as wide a selection of homes as possible. In the end, you should be the one to set limits.

Q. If we have no children, why would school districts matter to us?

A. If you intend to stay in your new home for a long time, a school district with a poor reputation might just give you a chance to pick up a bargain. But if you think you might be moving again within a few years, you could find it hard to resell. It's best, in that case, to look for a house that will appeal to the largest possible pool of potential buyers, including those who care about schools.

CHAPTER 3

Using a Buyer's (or a Seller's) Agent

When you walk into a store, you don't spend much time wondering about the status of the clerks who wait on you. You don't much care whether they are on salary or paid a commission on sales. You never stop to question whose interests they're putting first—yours, the store's, or their own.

But when you're engaged in what may be the biggest financial transaction of your life, all those questions are relevant. Whom does the agent work for? Whose interests come first? What services can you expect, and how does the law protect you?

Your whole homebuying experience will go more smoothly if you bone up on what is known as the Law of Agency.

All Those Different Words

For starters, it helps to keep straight the various terms for real estate licensees.

Agent is a general term for anyone empowered to act for another. Agents owe a special set of legal (*fiduciary*) duties to the persons who hired them (their *clients,* or *principals*). More on that all-important point later.

Broker is a legal term for someone licensed by the state to negotiate real estate transactions and to charge for services.

A *real estate salesperson* holds an entry-level state license, allowing that person to assist one specific broker, somewhat in the position of an apprentice. The broker is legally responsible for the salesperson's activities. (In some areas the word *agent* or *sales counselor* may be used for a salesperson, as opposed to a broker.) A salesperson may not operate without supervision and may not collect any fees except from the sponsoring broker, usually as a share of commissions earned by the salesperson's efforts.

REALTOR® is a trademarked designation (properly capitalized, like Band-Aid or Coke), used by a broker (in some areas a salesperson) who belongs to a private organization called the local Association or Board of REALTORS®, and also state and national associations. REALTORS® subscribe to a code of ethics that goes beyond state license law and often sponsor a local multiple-listing system that offers you access to houses listed for sale by many different firms.

REALTOR-ASSOCIATE® is the term used by some Boards of REALTORS® for salespersons who work under the supervision of member brokers.

So as you start your search for the best agent, do you prefer a salesperson or a broker? There's something to be said for each. In general, you can expect a broker to have had more education and experience. On the other hand, some long-time salespersons remain in that status simply because they prefer not to go into business for themselves. And you could run into a well-trained, highly motivated newcomer with the time and enthusiasm to do a first-class job for you.

Seller's Agent or Buyer's Agent?

In past years, brokers listed homes for sale, were legally committed to being the sellers' agents, owed special duties to sellers and dealt with buyers on that basis. Brokers were legally obligated, for example, to put the seller's interests first and, among other things, obtain the highest possible price for homes they had listed. That was true even if they were bringing buyers to houses listed by other brokers.

Often, though, brokers who were working with buyers tended to identify with the house-hunters and thus violated their fiduciary obligations to sellers. Many buyers also assumed that the agent with whom they were working was "their" broker, putting their interests first.

With the growth of the consumer movement, one state after another took action to raise buyers' awareness of just where they stood. In recent years some states have assumed that every broker was a seller's agent. Some states assume that every agent the buyer encounters is working for the buyer. Some states mandate that the broker is working for neither party. In every case, the new laws permit the status of the agent to be changed by agreement among the parties.

Find out whether the agent or salesperson you meet is legally obligated, in your state, to act in your best interest, or on behalf of sellers, or for no one.

In at least half the states, brokers are required to reveal, at first meeting, just whom they are working for. Often this involves a written disclosure of agency statement, and sometimes you, as a prospective buyer, must sign an acknowledgement that you understand the situation.

What Difference Does It Make?

The Law of Agency clearly sets out the broker's fiduciary duties to the *principal* (also known as the client), the one who retains the agent. Many people believe that the principal is the one who pays the agent, but that's not necessarily so, and it's not that simple.

The fiduciary duties are complex, but they boil down to one main point: The agent must put the principal's interest first, above anyone else's, including the agent's own concerns.

If you are asked to sign an acknowledgment that you know which side the agent is working for, don't just initial the notice without reading it. Insist that it be thoroughly explained to you. And consider how it will affect your purchase.

Agent's Fiduciary Duties

Take the trouble to learn what fiduciary duties mean, and how they apply to you. The main fiduciary duty an agent owes is complete *loyalty* to the principal that, strictly followed (it sometimes isn't), includes for the seller's agent obtaining the highest possible price for the property and never suggesting any offer under the listed price. A buyer's agent, on the other hand, is obligated to negotiate the purchase for the lowest possible price and to suggest offering prices that the agent thinks might be accepted.

☞ **Money-$aving Tip #8** *A buyer's agent is legally obligated to strive for the lowest possible purchase price.*

One duty owed a principal is *obedience* to the client's instructions, unless they are illegal. A seller's agent could not obey the instruction: "Keep quiet about our problems with the leaky roof." A buyer's agent could not obey the instruction: "Don't show us any house owned by a member of a minority group."

Any agent is required to keep the client's information *confidential*. This prohibits the seller's agent from sharing with you (the buyer) details of the seller's financial or family situation, unless of course the client has authorized such action. ("Facing foreclosure, seller desperate—make offer!") Whether the seller received previous offers, and for how much, would also be confidential information. A buyer's agent, on the other hand, may not reveal how high a price you would pay if you had to. A buyer's agent must keep your (the buyer's) information confidential, unless asked to conceal the fact that you aren't really financially able to go through with the deal—that, for example, you have a house to sell before you can buy, but you don't want that fact included in the contract.

Of particular importance to you as a buyer is the duty of *notice,* a duty that obliges the seller's agent to forward to the   ✳ principal any fact that would be in the seller's interest to know. If you are dealing with a seller's agent, never tip your hand during negotiations about how much you would really   ✳✳ pay for the property, because the agent is duty-bound to convey that news to the seller.

These duties are owed to the principal, the client. The third party—buyer or seller as the case may be—is considered to be in a different category, as a *customer*.

Duty Owed to a Customer

If you end up dealing with a seller's broker, remember that the law also protects you as a customer.

First, the seller's agent must be honest, straightforward and trustworthy with third parties. Your questions will receive honest answers, although sometimes an honest answer might be, "I can't answer that; I must keep the seller's financial information confidential."

Besides answering your questions honestly, sellers and their agents have an obligation to volunteer information about any serious (material) hidden defects you could not see for yourself. State laws differ, though, on whether they must also tell you about *stigmas,* past problems that don't techni-cally affect the real estate, like suicide or murder on the premises, illness of the seller and the like.

Next, you will receive a great deal of service paid for by the seller because, without this service to buyers, the prop-erty might never be sold.

And finally, you can take heart from the fact that if brokers didn't to some extent identify with the buyer, not much real estate would get sold!

If the agent is duty-bound to put the seller's interest first (and there's only one first place), how should this affect your relationship with a seller's broker? First, realize that no con-fidentiality is owed to you. It's only practical to reveal your financial situation if you expect to get effective service, but you may want to keep some information to yourself. Saying "but don't tell the seller" won't help because the agent does not have any special obligation of obedience to you. Never say anything to the seller's agent that you wouldn't say to the seller. Assume that whatever you say will be (or at least should be) passed on.

☞ **Money-$aving Tip #9** *Never tell a seller's broker how much you'll raise your offer for a particular house "if I have to."*

Second, take advantage of the fact that you must receive honest answers by asking questions. In some states you are entitled to a seller's written disclosure of defects, but else-where a good all-purpose query to ask of both seller and

broker, preferably in front of witnesses, is: "Are you aware   ✳
of any defects in this house?"

Hiring Your Own Broker

Until a few years ago, a buyer's broker was used only for
the purchase of commercial property. Today, however,
buyer representation is offered by many firms and is often
used for simple residential purchases.

To find a buyer's broker, simply ask real estate firms if they
offer that service. Often a lawyer who is active in real estate
can give you the names of a buyer's broker. You may also find
brokers who advertise their specialty in the yellow pages or
in real estate ads.

The buyer's agent may ask for a retainer to compensate for
time invested; sometimes the retainer applies against eventual commission due or even against the purchase price of
the property bought. If no property is bought within the
contracted time, the retainer may be forfeited.

Occasionally, the buyer pays the usual share (perhaps half)
of the commission originally promised a selling broker when
the house was listed for sale. In return, the seller may reduce
the sale price by that amount, because the seller will be
paying only half a full commission to the listing broker.

In theory the buyer who specifically hires a broker should
pay for the service. In real life, though, it usually works out
that the seller pays the originally agreed-upon commission,
part of which goes to the buyer's broker.

Why would the seller be willing to do that?

To help get the house sold.

Buyers, first-timers especially, don't have much spare cash
lying around when the sale closes. Just to make the deal work,
sellers are often willing to furnish the commission in that
fashion. In the same way, sellers sometimes pay "points"

charged by a bank (more on that in Chapter 9) just to help the buyer obtain a mortgage loan.

You will often hear, in that case, that the buyer's broker is to be paid "out of the proceeds of the transaction."

☞ **Money-$aving Tip #10** *Often the seller ends up paying the fee due to the buyer's broker.*

Proponents of the buyer's broker system like it because it sets up an adversary situation similar to that in which the parties retain two different attorneys. Sellers and buyers each have a broker clearly working for them alone, without the conflicts of interest that can arise under the more traditional system.

If you hire your own broker, you can expect to sign a contract in which you promise that during a specified period of time you will not house-hunt with anyone else and that if you buy any property within that time in any fashion, your broker will be entitled to a fee.

The contract should specify how the broker is to be paid— with a set fee, by the hour, or as a percentage of the house bought. It should specify what happens if a seller declines to pay your broker.

The system can work well. A buyer's broker is committed to helping you negotiate the lowest possible price, is free to point out drawbacks in any particular property, must keep your information confidential. But read any contract with a buyer's broker carefully before signing. If you don't like something, ask to have it changed.

A problem can arise with the system, though, if you find yourself tied to an agent who does not, in the end, suit your needs. It's well to remember that the old-fashioned method, in which you would deal entirely with sellers' brokers, has been around for years and can also bring satisfactory results.

Some sellers, willing to perform part of the brokerage work themselves, list their property with discount brokers, who offer limited services for a reduced commission. You need to understand the relationship because if you run into one, you as a buyer will also be expected to do part of the work by yourself. Most often, the broker saves time by making appointments but sending you to view houses on your own. You may be offered less help with mortgage financing. Because discount brokers usually belong to a multiple listing system, however, you can probably view their listed homes through other brokers.

Buying from a For Sale By Owner

Sellers who handle their own property are known as FSBOs (fizz-bo, "for sale by owner"). Some do it for the satisfaction of tackling an unaccustomed job, but they're not doing it just to pass on the saved commission to you. They usually plan to sell at fair market value and pocket the commission as extra profit in return for their efforts.

You will have extra work when you buy directly from an   ✷✸
owner. Unless you retain your own broker, you'll have to negotiate face to face, have extra attorney's input into the written contract, explore financing options on your own and ride herd on your own mortgage application process. It may be extra-important to have your own building inspector look the property over before you are committed.

You may want to buy from a FSBO if the place is unique, exactly what you want and haven't been able to find in listed properties. And sometimes you will run into a house that has been underpriced by a FSBO who chose to do without the services of an appraiser as well. In that situation, be prepared to act promptly; some investors lie in wait for unwary FSBOs and jump as soon as underpriced property hits the market.

Otherwise, it is usually a waste of energy to start your   ✷
house-hunting with FSBOs. Until you have a good grasp on prices in the area and the entire home-buying process, it can

be difficult to deal with homeowners who often have an exaggerated idea of a home's value and who don't know how to proceed. Wait until you, at least, know what you're doing—or hire a broker to represent you.

How the Agent Can Help

You agent should explain at first meeting who he or she represents. A seller's agent will treat you fairly and answer questions honestly. A buyer's agent will owe you the full range of duties, obey your instructions and keep your information confidential.

An agent can contact FSBOs for you and in many cases will be able to show you unlisted homes and represent you in negotiating for them.

Commonly Asked Questions

Q. Should I retain my own buyer's broker?

A. Part of the answer depends on your state's particular laws. In some places the agents you meet are already, legally, your representatives. Find that out right at the start.

Otherwise, you'd be well-advised to study the Law of Agency, learn the implications of the agent's duties and then decide for yourself. Remember that the old traditional system has worked pretty well for many years.

Although a seller's broker does not owe you those specific fiduciary duties, as a mere customer you are still entitled to honest, straightforward treatment and truthful answers to your questions, and you will still receive a great deal of service.

Q. Why does it have to be an adversarial situation? If they want to sell and I want to buy, why have opposing agents?

A. Many states do allow real estate licensees to act as *transaction brokers, facilitators* or *dual agents*. In such situations, the agent merely offers services and helps negotiate and facilitate the purchase and sale, without taking on either party as a client. Dual agency in particular, though, is a tricky situation and you should receive a careful explanation of what it implies.

CHAPTER 4

Finding the Best Agent for You

As with your search for the ideal veterinarian or hairdresser, recommendations from friends who have had a good experience may be the best way to find a good real estate agent. One caution, though: Brokers specialize. You want someone who concentrates on the area or type of house you're looking for.

Failing any recommendations that pan out, you will meet sellers' agents by answering advertisements, calling the phone numbers on lawn signs and visiting open houses. You can keep searching till you find someone who seems just right.

You have no legal obligations to a seller's agent, and you might be tempted to deal with several, so that you'll get many people out there looking for your dream house. In reality, though, the buyer who works with many brokers is working with no one. The broker who realizes you're house-hunting with others is not motivated to keep contacting you. In the absence of a legal relationship, many successful transactions flow from informal cooperation between buyer and broker. If you plan to use a seller's broker, when you find a good one stick with him or her.

Judging a Good Broker

Many of the following tests apply whether you're planning to retain a buyer's broker or to deal with a seller's agent.

First off, does the agent return phone calls promptly? This simple question is a good screening device, whether you're looking for a pediatrician or a plumber.

Then, does the agent explain things so you can understand them? This is especially important for first-time buyers. If you can find an agent who is a born teacher, you're in luck. (Actually, in fact, many brokers are former teachers.)

Does the agent seem ready to invest time in you? Where the broker is holding open a house that's on the market, for example, does he or she just wave you through, asking as you leave whether you're interested in the house and letting it go at that? You want someone who, if not busy with other prospects, shows you the house in a professional manner, asks questions about your needs and wants, offers to sit down and discuss other places on the market if you're not interested in this one.

Does the broker suggest an initial session in the office, rather than simply meeting you at the house you called about? To get good service, you need a financial analysis and discussion of your whole situation.

Does the agent ask questions about your finances soon after meeting you? These queries may not be good manners in ordinary society, but they will help the broker estimate what you can afford, and help you get it. Don't resent questions about your financial situation. They're the mark of an agent who intends to give you good service.

Does the broker alert you about his or her agency status and explain what's involved? In many states, you're entitled to this information upon first contact.

Do the first houses suggested show that the broker has been listening and understands your wants and needs? If you're shown houses with the wrong number of bedrooms, or clearly out of your price range, forget it.

Does the agent seem conversant with local conditions? Does he or she have maps of the area, handouts about schools, museums, property tax rates and the like?

Once you find a broker with whom you feel comfortable, one who inspires confidence, stick with him or her. Tell the broker about other firms' ads that interest you, even about FSBOs, so that the agent can investigate and report back to you. Ask for advice before visiting open houses on your own. If you have the agent's home phone number, don't hesitate to use it. Real estate agents are accustomed to evening and weekend calls. Service is the only thing they have to sell, and they welcome any sign that you intend to utilize it.

What about Lawyers?

Customs in real estate vary tremendously from one area to another, and in some locations you may be told that no one uses a lawyer, that legal work is handled by special escrow or title companies. The law does not require that you have legal counsel.

It is, nevertheless, usually foolish to proceed without professional help—your own attorney, entirely on your side. Lawyers are useful not so much for getting you out of trouble as they are for heading off trouble before it starts.

It's always wise to consult your own real estate attorney. Your lawyer will make sure the sales contract protects your interests, intervene if problems arise before closing and review final figures to make sure you get proper credit at settlement time.

Lawyers specialize just as physicians do. You don't want to end up with a corporate lawyer or a trial attorney for your house purchase. (In small towns, of course, most lawyers are generalists who handle real estate among many other matters.) To find a specialist, you can ask a broker to suggest two or three names. Agents know which attorneys are active in this field. In a strange town, you might call a bank and ask what firm handles its real estate work. Or you can call a large law firm and inquire which partner specializes in real estate.

Contact a lawyer early on. Call an attorney's office and explain that you're starting to house-hunt. If you don't feel comfortable with what you hear, shop around. And never hesitate to ask what the service is likely to cost.

If you are relocating to an area where lawyers are not routinely used for real estate purchases, discuss with your attorney just which services are needed beyond those provided by organizations like title or escrow companies.

If you are already paying for some legal services elsewhere, explain to your lawyer that you will need only limited help. Title search and guarantee, for example, may already be furnished by a title insurance company. It can still be valuable, however, to have your own attorney review your contract, clear up problems that may arise and go over closing figures at settlement.

Your lawyer will suggest the right time for further contact. If you have financial problems (judgments, etc.) that need clearing up, you may want legal input immediately. Otherwise you may not need to talk with the lawyer again until you are ready to make a written offer to purchase a specific property.

How the Agent Can Help

The average person assumes that a real estate agent's job is to help you find a house, but that's only the beginning. The typical broker will spend more time bringing you into agreement with the seller and, most important, will help you arrange to finance your purchase.

Even if you are using the seller's broker you can expect first an analysis of your financial situation. Don't be offended by what appear to be personal questions. A good agent asks them at the beginning because a lending institution will ask them later on. During a first conversation, the broker is already forming a strategy for financing your purchase, based on the various mortgage options outlined in Chapter 9.

Then you can look for basic real estate education. Brokers expect to spend extra time with first-time home buyers. You have a right to insist that every step be explained so that you feel comfortable.

Unless the broker recommends a specific price range, all of you—sellers, agents and you—are just wasting your time. It's useful to be told the price range for which you can qualify, but remember there's no need to reveal at this point the top price you're ready to pay.

If you'll be relocating, ask a local firm for help. Most franchise companies have efficient referral networks. Once connected, you will probably receive long-distance phone calls, maps, and offers to meet your plane, make motel reservations or arrange baby-sitting. Seeing the town with a broker as your chauffeur is one of the best ways to learn about neighborhoods, schools, shopping and the like.

The agent will show you any house that's on the market and must be careful not to narrow your choice by the use of subtle steering. A good agent, though, is a skilled matchmaker, who listens instead of talks and then helps you narrow down available listings for efficient use of your time.

The agent will set up appointments for house inspections and (unless a discount broker) will accompany you. During the tours, don't be afraid to ask questions. The agent will have at hand a wealth of data on each house you see, including lot size, property taxes and assessment figures, age of the house, square footage, heating system and the like.

When you are seriously interested in a specific house, the broker will sit down and help you figure out how you could buy it and what it would cost you each month.

The agent will prepare either a binding purchase contract or (in some areas) a preliminary memorandum of agreed terms. Differences between what you want and what the seller wants are negotiated until you and the seller reach what is known as a meeting of the minds.

If you are using an attorney, the broker works closely with the lawyer from the moment you make your first written offer to purchase.

Financing expertise is probably the most important and certainly the most time-consuming of the agent's activities. A skilled agent keeps in close touch with local lending institutions, and from among hundreds of different mortgage plans, helps you find the one that best suits you.

In many localities, the agent expects to make an appointment for you with a lending institution, help you prepare for the application interview, perhaps even accompany you. While you're waiting for loan approval, the agent will keep in touch with the lender to straighten out any hitches that develop.

Local customs vary, but in many areas the broker attends the closing session, and in a few places brokers actually effect the transfer of title.

Commonly Asked Questions

Q. Do I have to answer personal questions about money matters?

A. You do if you want good service. Not being frank is like going to a doctor and refusing to discuss your symptoms.

A seller's agent needs to know that you're qualified to buy before showing you specific houses, and your own buyer's agent is required by law to keep your information confidential.

It's particularly important to disclose past financial problems—judgments, even bankruptcy. There is often a way to overcome such problems, but you'll need help and advice to do so.

No law, though, says that you have to reveal everything. Once you've said enough to show you're financially able, there is no harm in keeping quiet about your total worth.

Q. What legal obligation do I have to stick with just one agent?

A. If you specifically retain your own buyer's broker, the terms of your agreement should be spelled out in writing. Often you may owe a commission to your broker even if you ended up buying through some other agent or directly from a FSBO.

If you are dealing with a seller's broker, you have no legal obligation and are free to work with any one you choose and to switch from one to another. For best service, though, it's best to stick with a single agent when you find one you like.

CHAPTER 5

Understanding How Much You Can Afford

Years ago, before credit cards had even been invented, the rule of thumb was that you could buy a house costing two and one-half times your annual income. The old guideline can still work if interest rates are around 10 percent, you can put 20 percent down, and you have few other debts. When rates are as low as 8 percent, you could plan on buying a house costing three times your income.

But otherwise it's not that simple. Interest rates fluctuate these days in a way that would have been unthinkable in bygone years. Current thinking concentrates on monthly costs of ownership as they compare with income and debts.

The process of determining how much it's safe for you to borrow is known as *qualifying*. Because a lending institution will qualify you when you are finally ready to apply for a mortgage loan, most good real estate brokers do it—usually with a written interview sheet—when they first meet you. This chapter will help you qualify yourself.

Debts Are Important Too

Your income is only the first factor in determining how much you can borrow. Equally important is the amount of your other financial obligations. Each lending institution and each mortgage plan has its own guidelines. Sometimes you are marked down for any long-standing debt that has more than six months to run, sometimes only for those with a full year or more to go. Outstanding student loans, life insurance payments, child support may affect your allowable mortgage payment, or they may not.

When reporting your income, include all the income of everyone who will be an owner of the house. Unmarried persons may pool their income to buy a house together just as a married couple can. If you are self-employed, average your past two years' income from that source. Include in your estimate all income from any source you can prove to a lending institution. Do not include one-time events like inheritances, insurance settlements and capital gains.

The term *underwriting* refers to the process of analyzing a mortgage application, looking over the paperwork exhibits (appraisal and/or inspection of the property, verification of employment, credit report, etc.) and making a decision about furnishing the loan. Underwriters decide which loans look safe and can be forwarded to their mortgage committees for approval.

The whole idea of the lender's analysis is to make sure you don't get in over your head with debt, which would put their mortgage loan in jeopardy. You could even be penalized for one problem you hadn't anticipated—the number of credit cards you presently carry. Even if you pay them off promptly and don't carry balances, if you have a whole collection of cards, lenders figure that you could go out tomorrow and borrow up to the hilt on all of them.

Particularly if your qualifications are borderline, that possibility might be enough to tip the scales against you. If you have half a dozen cards, consider officially closing most of those accounts as soon as possible.

Most lenders don't care about debts that will be paid off within six months (in some cases, 10 or 12 months), so when you list your debts, omit those with less than six months to go.

About Qualifying Ratios

Lenders figure your allowable mortgage payment many different ways. Some calculations even take into account your particular income tax payment and number of dependents. In general, though, you will hear about lending institutions' qualifying ratios. A typical ratio might be 28/36 or (more generous in the amount you could borrow) 29/41.

The first figure is the percentage of your gross monthly income the lender will allow as a maximum monthly payment. With a 28/36 ratio, you would be allowed to spend 28 percent of your monthly gross income on a mortgage payment. This is roughly "a week's income for a month's payment" because a month contains an average of 4.3 weeks.

Using a 28/36 ratio, a buyer with monthly gross income of $4,000 would be allowed up to $1,120 for a monthly mortgage payment. You can perform the calculation with your own income.

Lenders figure the allowable payment two different ways, however, and the next calculation takes into account your other current debts. The second figure in the ratio (36 percent) seems to allow a higher percentage of monthly income for mortgage payment, but that's because it must also cover other monthly debt payments.

The same buyer, with monthly gross income of $4,000, might have $400 in present debt payments. Applying the ratio (36 percent) yields $1,440 a month available for debt service. Subtracting present monthly payments of $400 qualifies the borrower for up to $1,040 in mortgage costs.

Lenders figure both ways, and then they take whichever figure is lower, more conservative. (That's why you don't want to go into debt for a new car while you're house-hunting.)

☞ **Money-$aving Tip #11** *You can walk into any real estate office and ask an agent to sit down and estimate how much you can spend for a home—at no cost and no obligation.*

Learn about PITI

The term PITI refers to the four figures that make up your monthly mortgage payment: Principal, Interest, Taxes and Insurance. With most mortgage plans, the lender will collect each month not only the first two items, but also one-twelfth of your yearly property taxes and your homeowner's insurance premium. Those tax and insurance bills will go directly to the lender, who will pay them with your money, put aside in a separate *escrow* or *trust* account. Lenders are concerned about those particular bills being met, to protect the security for their loan.

In the example given above, where $1,040 was the maximum PITI payment because the borrower had substantial other debts, how much could this buy?

For starters, how much mortgage loan could the borrower qualify for?

The answer is not simple.

Property taxes and insurance figures differ from one house to another. Interest rates differ from one mortgage plan to another. And, of course, the amount of cash available for down payment will make a difference. It's relatively simple to make the calculation when a particular house is already in mind. Nevertheless, you can get a rough estimate.

You'll need information (available from your agent) on average property tax bills in the price range and neighborhood you're aiming at. Homeowners insurance is a simpler matter, since the whole calculation is a rough estimate anyhow; $30 a month might be used. A wrong estimate won't make much difference there.

Assuming that property taxes average $2,400 a year in the neighborhood under consideration, the calculation on mortgage payment would run: $1,040 maximum payment, less $200 a month for taxes, less $30 a month for insurance, leaves $810 a month for principal and interest. You can run the calculation for yourself, using the lower of the two final figures from your earlier calculations.

Then the monthly payment table on page 46 should let you estimate how much you might borrow.

If our hypothetical buyers have $30,000 available for the down payment, and they can borrow $92,300, they can buy houses in the $122,300 range. For practical purposes, they could look anywhere under $135,000, because one never knows what sellers will take, and the whole calculation is rough anyhow, until exact property taxes and interest rates are known.

Picking a Mortgage Plan

Your mortgage payment will almost certainly be your largest single expense. It is for most people. If you buy when interest rates are relatively low, you will probably opt for a fixed-rate mortgage. In that case, you can calculate at the start exactly what you'll pay each month for principal and interest for perhaps 15, 25 or 30 years.

When interest rates climb, more borrowers choose adjustable-rate mortgages. If you know the lifetime cap or ceiling

Monthly Payment for Each $1,000 Borrowed			
Number of Years on the Loan			
15	**20**	**25**	**30**
Interest Rate (%) 5			
7.91	6.60	5.85	5.37
6	8.44	7.17	6.45	6.00
7	8.99	7.76	7.07	6.66
7½	9.28	8.06	7.39	7.00
8	9.56	8.37	7.72	7.34
8½	9.85	8.68	8.05	7.69
9	10.14	9.00	8.39	8.05
9½	10.44	9.33	8.74	8.41
10	10.75	9.66	9.09	8.78
10½	11.05	9.99	9.45	9.15
11	11.37	10.33	9.81	9.53
12	12.00	11.02	10.54	10.29
13	12.65	11.72	11.28	11.07

on your interest rate, you can calculate the worst case right at the beginning–the highest monthly charge you could ever have if interest rates shot through the roof some time during the term of your loan.

☞ **Money-$aving Tip #12** *When interest rates are low, go for a fixed-rate mortgage. In years to come, as income, cost of living, interest rates and prices rise, your stable payment will become more and more of a bargain.*

The next two items in the standard PITI payment are taxes and insurance, which can be handled in one of two ways. You may meet those bills on your own, or—more likely—they will be handled for you by the lending institution.

Why the Escrow Account?

If your home were ever seized and sold for unpaid back taxes, the lending institution would be left with no security for its mortgage because a tax sale wipes out mortgages on the property. If the house burned to the ground, only the vacant lot would remain as security. Or, if you're located in a flood plain, your house could conceivably be swept away with not even the land left. So your lender has a direct interest in seeing that you pay your taxes and insurance premiums on time.

With most mortgages, including all VA and FHA loans, an escrow account (reserve, impound, trust account) is set up for you by the lender. Each month, along with your principal and interest payment, you send along one-twelfth of your anticipated next property tax and homeowner's insurance (sometimes, flood insurance) costs. As the bills come due, they are sent to your lender, who pays them on your behalf.

Your lender is allowed to keep not only enough to pay the next bill due, but also a two-month surplus as a precaution.

☞ **Money-$aving Tip #13** *In about half the states, you are entitled to interest on your escrow account.*

You will receive regular reports, monthly or at the end of the year, on the status of the escrow account, which is, after all, your own money. At regular intervals, usually yearly, the account will be analyzed and your payment adjusted, up or down, depending on whether the account shows a surplus or deficit.

Even with a fixed-rate mortgage, be prepared for annual payment adjustments to provide for changes in property taxes and homeowners' insurance premiums. These adjustments can be a surprise to the homeowner with a fixed-interest mortgage, who expected monthly payments to remain at exactly the same amount for the full term of the loan. It is, of course, taxes and insurance costs that change, not—with a fixed-interest loan—the underlying principal and interest portion of the payment.

About Homeowners Insurance

If you want a mortgage loan, you'll have to keep insurance on your property. You must prove that you've bought insurance before they'll turn the mortgage check over to you to pay the seller, and you must name the lender as an interested party on the policy. If you are not required to maintain an escrow account (that's sometimes possible), you can pay the premiums on your own, but the lender is usually entitled to proof, every year, that the bills have been paid.

The mortgagee (lender) will require that you keep what is known as hazard insurance (fire and similar risks) on the property in an amount sufficient to cover the loan. As a prudent homeowner, you will want wider coverage, and for a larger amount. Rebuilding after a fire, even partially, can sometimes cost more than your original purchase price. And you need personal protection for risks that don't concern your lender—liability for a guest who is hurt on your property, for example.

Your best bet is a homeowner's policy that puts many kinds of insurance together in a package. A basic homeowner's policy provides reimbursement for the most common forms of loss. The least expensive, called basic or HO (homeowner's)-1, covers fire, windstorm, explosion, smoke, glass breakage and other perils, including three very important ones: theft, vandalism and liability.

More expensive is the broad form, HO-2, which adds several more items, largely connected with plumbing, heating and electrical systems. HO-3, comprehensive insurance (all-risk), covers even more items and is considered a luxury item. HO-6, which covers the contents of your unit, is used for condominiums, townhouses and cooperatives. State regulations dictate the specific coverage in the various policies.

Besides asking what is covered by the policy you buy, it's important to find out what is not covered (earthquakes, floods, falling objects from airplanes). If you have a valuable collection or expensive jewelry, you may want to pay an additional premium for riders covering those items.

One way to economize on insurance cost is to opt for a larger deductible. This is the portion of your loss you agree to pay yourself. You wouldn't want the bother of filing claims for $250 losses in any event, and you're not buying insurance as a money-making proposition. Agreeing to handle a larger amount of any loss on your own can cut premiums considerably. Insurance is intended to cover real catastrophes, the kind you couldn't handle yourself. Investigate the relative costs at different deductible levels. You may also be able to save money if you buy homeowners insurance and auto or life insurance from the same company.

☞ **Money-$aving Tip #14** *You can save considerably on your homeowners insurance policy by agreeing to pay small claims on your own.*

Aim for Replacement Value

Suppose your ten-year-old roof is damaged by fire so badly that it must be completely rebuilt. How much is it fair for the insurance company to pay you?

You will end up with a brand-new roof instead of the old one, which was halfway through its useful life. It could be argued that you are entitled to only half the cost of a new roof. On the other hand, you can't buy a half-used roof; you must spend the money now for a completely new one. To forestall this problem, make sure that your insurance policy will pay you full replacement value in case of loss.

If your house is located in what the federal government considers a flood-prone area according to official maps, you'll have to carry flood insurance before you can get a mortgage loan from a regular lending institution. If flood insurance is difficult to obtain, you can buy it through a federal government program. This requirement can sometimes be dropped, though, if you can submit a survey showing that the lowest part of your building is above the 100-year flood mark.

☞ **Money-$aving Tip #15** *If your building itself is above the flood plain, sometimes you can avoid otherwise-mandatory flood insurance.*

Even though a condo association carries insurance on its building, you should still carry your own. Though you may feel you own little of value, you might be hard put to replace your stereo set, computer, VCR and TV at the least. Special homeowner's insurance is available for individual condominium units.

If you are presently renting, give serious consideration to renter's insurance. Renter's insurance is a useful way to protect against loss of your personal belongings. Your landlord's policy does not cover your possessions. Renter's insurance is relatively inexpensive.

An insurance agent may represent one company or may be an independent broker who places your policy with any one of several companies. Most important, perhaps, is that the agent be able to explain things so that you understand exactly what kind of protection you are buying.

About Property Taxes

In some areas, property taxes remain the same when ownership of a house is transferred, and you can be sure that the tax bill the seller received last year will be the one you receive next year, except for any community-wide increases. In other areas, the assessment (valuation of the house for tax purposes) changes to reflect your purchase price. Next year's taxes would be based on that figure. It's a simple matter to inquire which system is followed in the areas you are considering.

Make sure you know the true tax figure on any house you are considering buying. The present owner may have some   *
tax abatement; various possibilities, which differ from one state to another, include a senior citizens' discount, veterans' tax exemption, and preferential treatment for religious organizations.

On the other hand, the seller's tax figure may be higher than the true tax figure. In some localities, for example, unpaid water bills are added to the tax bill. On rare occasions a seller who neglects property could have costs for grass-cutting and even repairs by the city added to the tax bill.

The true tax figure has none of these exemptions or additions. It is the amount an average homeowner would pay on the property. Ask the broker whether the figure has been checked. Property taxes are a matter of public record, and you could call the taxing authorities yourself to inquire whether the current tax bill is a *true tax* figure or whether it   *
reflects some unusual adjustments.

Find out whether taxes in your state are paid in advance, for the coming fiscal year, or in arrears, at the end of the tax year. If you are considering a brand-new house, remember that present taxes are probably based on the value of the   *
vacant lot only, not the lot and house. The exact amount you will be paying may or may not be established at the time you

buy. You can always inquire of the local tax department approximately how much that would be.

☞ **Money-$aving Tip #16** *Be sure you know the true tax figure on any property you consider buying.*

Cash for Your Purchase

Besides your down payment and any points you may pay (see Chapter 9), you will need cash on the day you actually buy the property for what are known as closing costs. The agent can help you with a rough estimate of what you'll be expected to pay. You will owe some of the following: lender's attorney's fee and your own if you are using one, title insurance, prepaid mortgage insurance premium for FHA or PMI (private mortgage insurance), VA guarantee fees, impound or escrow deposits to fund your escrow account, origination fees, recording fees, your buyers' broker's commission (which may, however, be paid by the seller "out of the proceeds of the transaction.")

With certain mortgage plans, it is possible for a willing seller to agree to cover some of your closing costs. If you're short on cash, that would be one matter for negotiation when you're arriving at a binding purchase contract.

In addition, you will already have spent money for a mortgage application (to cover credit checks and appraisal of the property) and as you near the day of closing, home-owners insurance and in some cases, flood insurance.

Other Costs of Owning

For any house you consider, find out whether trash collection is included in taxes, and whether there is any extra charge for services like sidewalk snowplowing. Inquire about sewer and water charges. Ask the sellers about their utility and fuel bills for the past year or, better yet, for two years back.

Some authorities recommend setting aside 2 percent of purchase price for annual maintenance. It's impossible, of course, to set any rule, since the age and present condition of houses vary so widely.

Include in your calculation of monthly costs the price of basic telephone service and, for most households, cable TV; those figures may vary from one locality to another. Compare costs on homes you may be considering.

How the Agent Can Help

Besides helping with your house-hunting, the agent will help with your financial planning all along the way. The service starts with that initial analysis, to estimate what price range you could afford.

Then as you begin to narrow down your choice, the agent can furnish a rough guide to the amount of money needed to purchase a specific house, and your approximate monthly carrying costs.

Agents can tell you the average tax bill in the price range and neighborhoods you're interested in, help you estimate homeowners insurance costs, give you the exact property tax figure on any house you're interested in.

Although they are not engineers or home inspectors, most agents can give you a rough idea of how much might be needed to correct roof, heating or plumbing problems.

Commonly Asked Questions

Q. *Why is it anyone else's business if we think we can afford to buy?*

A. Lending institutions are required by law to be careful about how they lend out funds. They need reassurance that you pay your bills on time and that you will have enough income to pay them or enough assets to draw upon if times get hard. That's why you must give them proof by revealing what you may consider private information about your finances.

Q. *Must we reveal all that if we're prepared to buy for all cash?*

A. In such a situation, the seller would probably ask for proof that you have the purchase money available, before accepting your offer. You'd certainly be entitled to keep anything else about your finances private.

Q. *What can we do if we have good income and credit but little cash available?*

A. Look for a low-down-payment mortgage plan (see Chapter 9) and have the agent try to arrange for the seller to pay part of your closing costs.

Q. *How much is the lender allowed to keep in my escrow account?*

A. One-twelfth of your property tax and insurance costs for each month since the last payment, and a two-month cushion in addition.

CHAPTER 6

Choosing the Right Type of House

Just as important as your choice of neighborhood, and probably dictating your selection of areas for your search, is the type of home you want.

For most buyers, house-hunting involves looking at pre-owned single homes, sometimes referred to as previously lived-in or existing houses, which will be discussed in the following chapter. You may, however, prefer a brand-new home, either already built and ready, or customized to your specifications. If you prefer apartment living but want to own your home, you can consider condominiums, cooperatives and townhouses. Or you may want to buy a mobile home, properly referred to these days as manufactured housing.

Buying a Brand-New Home

If you want a brand-new house, you have a choice of three options. You can buy your own lot and hire your own contractor. You can deal with a builder who is developing a tract of land. Or—most difficult from many aspects—you can become a self-builder, doing some of the work yourself and serving as your own general contractor.

Having a house custom-built to one's own specifications is a favorite daydream for many people. The chance to pick the right lot, site the house as you want, create an environment that reflects your taste and personality is a seductive thought.

No matter which route you go, however, be aware that everything will take longer than expected; everything will cost more than expected; the weather will turn uncooperative; changing your mind about anything as you go along will be amazingly expensive; your marriage will be strained by constant decisions and different points of view; and even with the best general contractor, large amounts of your own time and attention will be required.

Buying a Separate Lot

If you are not buying into a new development or tract, take special precautions as you select your land. Find out about local regulations for minimum lot size and road frontage. In the suburbs or out in the country, investigate the availability of water, sewer, electric and gas service. If you will use a septic tank, be sure your purchase contract states that you will complete the transaction only if the land passes a percolation test. Your contract should not become binding until you receive all necessary local permits for building.

Using an Architect

Architects, who are often paid by a percentage of total construction cost, can more than earn their charges. An architect will do much more than help design the house you want and, in conjunction with your contractor, furnish a preliminary cost estimate. Brought in early enough, the architect can advise on siting of the building and possible drainage problems on various lots you are considering. In addition to your design, you need plans and specifications, and if you are letting the work out to bid, help with that process.

An architect's services go far beyond drawing up plans. An architect will assist with the paperwork needed for local permits, oversee the contractor's work as the building progresses, serve as a buffer between you and the workmen if problems arise.

Using a Contractor

Among the details you must check on: Does the general contractor carry proper insurance? Is the contractor paying subcontractors as agreed? Are local authorities making the necessary inspections as various phases of construction are completed?

To take care of problems that may surface soon after you move in, arrange for your final payment to be held by a third party in escrow. The builder or contractor should receive that last installment only after you are satisfied that everything has been completed as promised.

Self-Building

If you plan to build the house yourself, hiring subcontractors only for work you cannot do—excavation, for example— the first big challenge you'll run up against is financing. Because vacant land produces no income and can be difficult to resell, lending institutions almost never lend on land. You'll have to pay cash for your lot or find a seller willing to hold a mortgage.

Then, because lenders don't want the risk of being left with a half-finished problem on their hands, finding a building loan will also be difficult. It can be almost impossible to obtain institutional financing for self-building. In the end, you will probably be limited by whatever cash you have available. As a self-builder, be sure to consult your insurance agent about proper coverage.

Buying in a Development

You are likely to get more house for your money if you build in a tract already being developed. Paperwork and financing will be much simpler. You can see a model of the house you'll eventually own, and you're not likely to end up with cost overruns. You usually have some choices in items like kitchen cabinets and carpeting. (While you cannot usually negotiate on price, you can sometimes hold out for free upgrades on fixtures.)

The major drawback to buying in a development is the danger that it won't develop as promised. You are dependent on the developer's financial health and the success of the whole project.

Buying an Apartment

In areas where land is at a premium, cooperatives and condominium apartments may be an attractive alternative to more expensive housing. Many empty-nesters and busy young professionals also enjoy the absence of outside chores. It's easy to just lock the door and travel without worrying. Such apartments combine the advantages of home-owning with the convenience of apartment living. The Internal Revenue Service treats cooperatives and condominiums exactly as it does single family houses.

Cooperatives

The *cooperative* is the older form of ownership, found mainly in New York City, Chicago and a few other areas. The owner of a cooperative does not own any real estate. Rather, the buyer receives two things: shares in a corporation that owns the entire building and a proprietary lease for the particular living unit being bought.

Because a large part of the monthly charge goes toward property taxes and interest on the underlying mortgage, the prospective buyer can expect a certain percentage of that expenditure to be income tax deductible at the end of the year. If you are interested in a cooperative, you will be told what percent of the monthly charge is deductible. Inquire also about the dollar amount of liability you will be taking on for your share of the existing mortgage on the whole building. This will be in addition to any loan you place to buy your shares.

☞ **Money-$aving Tip #17** *The IRS allows deduction of property taxes and loan interest payments for cooperatives and condominiums just as it does for single homes.*

Cooperative shares and the lease are classified not as real estate but as personal property. They may be borrowed against, however, to assist with the purchase, and the IRS will treat the loan as if it were a mortgage. The owner of a cooperative does not owe any property tax on the individual living unit. Instead, the monthly payment includes a share of taxes paid by the cooperative on the entire building. It also includes a share of the cooperative's payment on the one large mortgage on the entire building, as well as the usual maintenance costs.

Tenant-owners in a cooperative building are dependent on each other for financial stability. For that reason, most coop-

eratives require that prospective buyers be approved by the
board of directors.

Condominiums

The term *condominium* describes a form of ownership,
rather than—as is usually assumed—an apartment. The buyer
of a condominium receives a deed and owns real estate, just
as a single house would be owned. In the case of a condominium, the buyer receives complete title to the interior of
the apartment ("from the plaster in") and also of a percentage
of the common elements—the land itself, staircases, sidewalks, swimming pool, driveways, lawns, elevators, roofs,
heating systems.

The condominium is classified as real estate, and the buyer
may place a mortgage on the property and will receive an
individual tax bill for the one unit. In addition, monthly fees
are levied to pay for outside maintenance, repairs, landscaping or snow removal, recreation facilities and the like.

Townhouses

Architecturally, a *townhouse* is an attached, usually up-
and-down house of the sort known in some cities as a row
house. In recent years, however, it also describes a type of
ownership.

Townhouse developments are a hybrid form of condominium and/or cooperative and can take many forms. Typically,
the unit owner has fee simple (complete) ownership of the
living space and the land below it, with some form of group
ownership of common areas. The individual may or may not
own a small patio or front area, may or may not own the roof
above the unit. As with an old-fashioned row house, there is
usually no other unit above the townhouse.

Common areas are owned by a homeowners association, and several different forms of legal organization are possible. As with condominiums, monthly fees may be levied to pay for the maintenance of the common areas.

Questions To Ask

Be sure to ask about parking: How far from your unit will it be, and are you entitled to more than one space? Where will your guests park? It's helpful to get this information in writing.

Before buying any type of apartment, you should be furnished with a daunting amount of material to read. Look all of it over carefully. Enlist the aid of an accountant and/or attorney to review the material.

What is the financial health of the organization you will be joining? Does it have substantial reserves put aside to cover major renovations and replacements? Ask about the condition of the building(s). Is there likely to be a need soon for new roofing, elevators, boilers, windows, for which you would bear a share of responsibility?

☞ **Money-$aving Tip #18** *Investigate the financial health of the condo, cooperative or townhouse organization you would join.*

Ask whether any special assessments are expected in the near future. It helps if you can get a written answer to this one, or at least something in front of witnesses. If all the skylights have been leaking recently, or chimneys need tuck-pointing, you might find yourself hit with an unexpected bill soon after you move in.

Study the covenants, conditions and regulations you must promise to observe. Could you rent out your apartment, install awnings, paint your front door red, plant tomatoes anywhere, eventually sell the unit on the open market?

Find out the percentage of owner-occupancy. More home-owners and fewer tenants is the preferred situation. On the other hand, would you have the right to sublet if you needed to?

What about Mobile Homes?

Once known as trailers, then officially renamed as mobile homes, now properly referred to as manufactured housing, these homes can be a good option, depending in large part on your geographical location. Investigate whether in your community mobile homes represent a good investment or merely a convenient way to live. In many areas, particularly in the South and West, mobile homes are a way of life for a large proportion of the population. One attraction is lower initial cost, as compared with a completely furnished single home.

One problem is finding the lot on which you can put your mobile home; some communities are zoned against them. Many mobile homes therefore are placed on rented land; they are classified as personal property rather than as real estate.

If the home is on a foundation and on its own land, it does count as real estate. Out in the country, it's likely to use a septic system. When house-hunting, be sure to ask some specific questions about the system's capacity and overall health.

Picking the mobile home community into which you buy may be more important than picking the individual home itself. Talk with occupants of the development; find out how cooperative and well-staffed the management is. Although the home is yours, to some extent you will be a tenant, and a fairly captive one, because mobile homes are often not very mobile, and you are not likely to move yours to another location.

Give some consideration to buying a used mobile home. Brand-new ones in some areas depreciate in value like brand-new automobiles. You may pick up a bargain in a used one and stand a better chance of recouping your investment or even—in a choice development—seeing some profit when you turn around and sell in the future.

The right mobile home can be a pleasant and relatively inexpensive way of living, but it will almost never appreciate in value as a site-built house would. Used mobile homes compete with brand-new ones full of brand-new furniture and appliances when it's time to resell, and that puts a limit on their value.

How the Agent Can Help

Real estate brokers handle vacant land, mobile homes, condominiums, townhouses and cooperative apartments as well as single detached houses. An agent can orient you to the local market for these different types of homes.

Particularly in a rural area, the agent should have information on building regulations and about the paperwork process for building approval.

Developers and builders, though they may not enter their houses in a local multiple listing system, often do cooperate with agents. If you are interested in a particular tract, the broker you are working with can contact the developer and can often help negotiate your purchase contract. The sale price usually remains the same even if some commission will be paid.

Commonly Asked Questions

Q. We found a condo we'd like to buy, but we plan to rent it out part of the year, and we're told we'd have to pay a special fee to the Homeowners Association. Can they really charge that?

A. Many condo developments try to discourage renting out of their apartments, on the theory that a large number of tenant-occupied units can hurt the health of the organization. Some lending institutions refuse to make mortgage loans in buildings where too many apartments are rented out. You are being properly warned in advance about the extra fees you might incur, and you're always free not to buy if you don't like the rules.

Q. Does a mobile-home community have the right to forbid occupancy by children?

A. Unless the community meets specific requirements as a senior citizen development, such a restriction violates fair housing laws.

Q. Can the agent we've been working with help us in the purchase of a brand-new home?

A. Probably. Most developers these days understand the position of a buyer's broker and welcome inquiries from your agent. If you have been working with an old-style seller's broker, that person can still make the first approach to a builder for you.

Q. As first-time buyers, we're attracted to a new mobile home, completely furnished. It seems like a good way to start. Is it?

A. The answer depends on your situation and your location. Buying a mobile home can be a simple attractive way to start out, but in many parts of the country the drawbacks become apparent after a few years. Living in a mobile home with a couple of toddlers becomes difficult, and the young couple who want to move may find that they owe more on their loan than they can sell the home for.

Q. If we build the home ourselves, how do we figure the value of our time in arriving at our cost basis for income tax purposes?

A. Your cost basis will include the price of your lot, any material you paid for and any actual cash outlay for other person's labor. You cannot include anything for your own time or anything you did not actually pay for.

Q. Are mobile homes ever a good investment?

A. Older homebuyers who expect to remain there well into the future and empty-nesters who choose a good mobile home development in a retirement community are more likely to find their homes become good long-term investments.

CHAPTER 7

Winning by Careful House-Hunting

As you begin your house-hunting, your first step will probably be to narrow down your choice of towns, suburbs or neighborhoods. Don't overlook the matter of commuting time.

Not many of us enjoy a long daily commute, so as you consider your choice of areas for house-hunting, it can be helpful to try them out for commuting time. For a few days, try driving home from work to several different locations, so you can judge. Remember that while you can change the condition or layout of the house you buy, you won't be able to change the neighborhood.

Viewing houses on the market can be hard work. If you look at more than four in a morning or afternoon, you'll end up with your head in a whirl. Make the job as pleasant and exciting as possible by preparing carefully. Older children, facing the upheaval of a move, may enjoy being involved in your house-hunting. But taking along infants and toddlers makes it difficult to concentrate on the job at hand. Try to arrange baby-sitting whenever possible.

Do take a street map of the community, highlighters to mark the location of various houses, a notebook or clipboard and pen, and a tape measure. An instant camera is useful (often an agent has one or can borrow one from the office.)

Ask the agent for data on each property, and take it back with you. In order to concentrate fully on the house, wait to make notes until you have finished, possibly when you are back in the car. Jot down your impressions right on the computer printouts or copies of the listing sheets for the houses you inspect.

If you then note the things you disliked about the place or which features really appeal to you, sorting it out later becomes easier. Mark up your street map, locating not only the houses you view but also noting schools, religious institutions, shopping areas and other amenities.

Pay Attention to Layout

While you can change the condition of the house you buy, it can be expensive or impossible to change the layout. Remember a few basics as you inspect houses.

For any house you are seriously considering, imagine yourself going about the daily routine. When you come home with a load of groceries, where will you park? Will you have to carry the load up stairs? Must you go through the living room? Is there a handy counter near the refrigerator for unloading?

Imagine yourselves in midsummer, eating out on the enclosed porch, patio or deck. Will it be easy to serve from the kitchen, without risking spills on the living room carpet en route?

A small enclosed front foyer allows a thermostat to be shielded from icy blasts, or in summer, from waves of hot air.

The guest entrance should have a handy coat closet, and ideally a nearby powder room or half-bath.

Kitchen Layout

Check the kitchen for sufficient counter and cupboard space. Double-check for a place to put things down, not only next to the refrigerator but also at the stove and sink. Consider traffic moving through the kitchen; it should not disrupt the refrigerator-sink-stove work area.

Even if you are resigned to a small Pullman kitchen and plan to eat in the dining room, look for enough space for a high chair, or a stool for a chatty guest.

If the family includes small children, the kitchen windows should overlook play areas.

☞ **Money-$aving Tip #19** *Pay attention to floor plans; changing layouts of rooms later can be costly.*

Other Layout Considerations

Ideally, you should not have to go through the living room to reach other areas. A dead-end living room makes for relaxation and tends to stay neat. Check whether bedrooms are separated by sound barriers like hall or closets. Consider, in a one-floor layout, whether you can get from bedrooms to bath without being observed from the more public areas. Look for the convenience of an outside entrance to the basement and a small outside door to the garage.

Looking for Bargains

Housekeeping

Number one on your list of bargain opportunities should be a house that suffers from bad housekeeping. The grass hasn't been cut, the porch light doesn't work, the windows are dirty—and that's even before you enter the front door. Inside, the front closet is overflowing, no one has turned off the television set in the living room, and you stumble over children's toys in the hall. And the mess just gets worse as you go through the property. When you locate such a house, if it has had decent maintenance (as opposed to housekeeping), then you have stumbled upon a bargain. Houses that have been rented out sometimes fall into this category.

Most buyers cannot see past sloppiness. Perhaps without even knowing why, they say that "The place doesn't have good vibes." As a result, the house may stay on the market for months and will probably sell for as much as 10 percent under true market value.

☞ **Money-$aving Tip #20** *Try to ignore sloppy housekeeping and concentrate on basic condition; that's one way to find a bargain.*

On the other hand, as you walk into a spotless house, try to ignore the smell of pot roast wafting through the place, the music playing softly and the bowl of polished apples or vase of flowers on the hall table. Of course such a house has probably had fine care, and it could be a pleasure to move into. Still, when the sellers move out they will take the table, the CD player, those great speakers and the pot roast. You will be left with just three things: the location, layout and condition.

If those factors—apart from surface appeal—seem right to you, don't hesitate about putting in your offer for such a house. It will sell quickly. If it's also been underpriced, emergency action is indicated, as described in the next chapter. More commonly, a house that shows well commands a premium.

When it comes to decorating and housekeeping, try to ignore cosmetics and concentrate on basics. Location can't be changed, floor plan can be altered only at some expense, but the last factor—condition—can be remedied. Just be sure, if there's a problem, that you know what you're getting into. An engineering report, as discussed in Chapter 8, can tell you exactly what to expect.

Seller under Pressure

Bargains can also be found where sellers are under pressure. The seller's broker won't (or shouldn't at any rate) reveal that the house is near foreclosure or the seller is going bankrupt. But you can see for yourself sometimes, if it's a divorce situation, if the house is vacant or doesn't look lived-in, if one parent is on a new job in Santa Fe and the other is here alone with three kids and big long-distance phone bills. Such sellers may be ready to deal and ready to trade a price concession for a quick sale.

☞ **Money-$aving Tip #21** *Find out all you can about the seller's situation, to help you in price negotiations.*

Other Sources for Bargains

Where the owner has died, an executor is sometimes amenable to any reasonable offer in return for a prompt, trouble-free winding up of the estate. An older person, suspicious of workers and short on cash, may not want to bring a long-time home up to standards required by a lending institution; sometimes a broker can help you work out a mutually beneficial arrangement to solve that impasse.

Above all, the way to buy a bargain is to buy promptly. The buying public is a sensitive judge of value. A house that is mistakenly underpriced will be snapped up quickly. For that reason, it's sensible to invest some time in learning the market and helpful to locate a broker in whose advice you have confidence.

Neighborhood Affects Value

Before you are very far into your house-hunting, someone will tell you the oldest real estate joke (almost the only real estate joke): The three most important factors in the value of a house are (1) location, (2) location and (3) location.

It's true, too. A house costing $600,000 in Beverly Hills might sell, on a comparable lot in the suburbs of Peoria, for $100,000. Never in the history of this country have locational differences been so marked. Closer to home, you know yourself that a modest home in the most expensive suburb is worth much more than the identical house in an inner-city neighborhood.

From a buyer's point of view, there are two ways of looking at this locational preference. The classic advice is to buy the modest house on a more expensive street. Such a house is easy to resell, and its value will hold up well, for there are always buyers eager for the prestige of that particular neighborhood. And remodeling or adding to it is possible because alterations won't push it out of the price range for that area.

The most luxurious house on the street, on the other hand, won't ever repay the owner for the money invested. No matter how elegant it may be, buyers with money to spend will aim at a different, more prestigious neighborhood.

In one way, then, an overimproved house represents an opportunity for the buyer who wants lots of space and luxury features and isn't worried about resale value. If you think you will live in the house for a long time, and if you like the area, you may be able to pick up a great deal for your money.

☞ **Money-$aving Tip #22** *Remember that the best house on the street can be hard to sell, or to resell.*

Before you invest in a home, though, pay attention to the trend in the neighborhood. One that's on its way down could pose real problems when you go to sell. On the other hand, an up-and-coming area can prove a good investment. You can judge by the exterior of nearby houses. Are they being allowed to run down—missing spindles on porch railings, junk cars in driveways? Or are there signs of revitalization— new paint jobs, roofers at work? Local police can give you statistics on whether crime rates are rising or falling in a given area, and you can learn a lot about the schools by attending a meeting of the local PTA.

Judging Condition

Always ask the seller directly, or if that's not possible, the seller's agent, about hidden defects in the house. For any house you're seriously considering, ask about heating and cooling costs, charges for water, type and amount of insulation, trash removal, age of the roof. Even where sellers furnish a written disclosure of condition, try to ask sellers directly if there are defects you can't see for yourself.

If you're buying a brand-new house, investigate the builder's reputation. Walk through completed areas and chat with owners to find out whether the builder makes prompt repairs on any early defects. Be sure to read the bylaws of any homeowners association.

Condition of an Older Home

If you want to buy an older home, you will probably use the services of a home inspector but you won't want that expense for every house you're considering. It's worth doing a little preinspecting yourself.

In general, houses built since World War II are more or less modern. In these, you can pretty much count on copper plumbing, adequate electric service and a furnace that is at least compact. Houses more than 20 years old, however, require extra-careful inspection. You won't look in detail at every house you see, but when you're seriously considering making an offer on one, go over it carefully.

Start with the outside of the house. Does it have easy-care features—built-in sprinklers in a dry climate or self-storing storm windows up north? How soon might the place need a coat of paint?

Examine the roof; binoculars can be of help here. Look for missing or curled shingles, patched spots or a dried-up, crinkled appearance. Moss growing on the roof indicates a moisture problem. A roof clear of snow after a snowstorm may indicate a house with inadequate insulation.

In termite areas (Southeast, Southwest), look for mud tubes where wooden parts of porch or foundation adjoin the ground. Poke exposed wood to see if it is solid.

In some Northern areas termites are just about unheard-of, but you might find carpenter ants. Look for small piles of fine sawdust below ceiling beams. Prod floor joists, if they are exposed in the cellar, to check for soft spots.

Downspouts should be firmly attached. If gutters need only repainting, that's a minor matter, but gutters with holes in them will need replacing.

The homeowners' warranty a seller may furnish looks reassuring, and it can't do any harm. Don't pick your house just because one is offered, however. Those policies do not usually cover structural defects, and they may have high deductibles, so that you'd have to pay on your own if a repair was needed.

Electric Service and Plumbing

Many homes built around the turn of the century didn't originally have any electric service. If the initial installation hasn't been updated, it can be inadequate for anything beyond the light bulbs, refrigerator and flatiron it was originally designed for. The proliferation of appliances these days calls for plenty of outlets. You want 100-amp service at a minimum and 220-amp for electric stoves and some clothes dryers and air conditioners. Look for an outlet every 12 feet on a long wall, so that any six-foot cord can be plugged in without using an extension cord. Small rooms should have at least one outlet on each wall.

Upstairs, be alert for any tangle of extension cords; it can be symptomatic of inadequate outlets. Downstairs, examine the fuse box. If you find circuit breakers, you will know that the service has been modernized. But there is nothing wrong with an old-fashioned fuse system, if it is extensive enough and was carefully installed.

More expensive to remedy than inadequate wiring is faulty plumbing. You hope to find all the old galvanized pipes replaced with copper. Galvanized pipe suffers from corrosion and eventually develops hardening of the arteries, where deposits narrow down the inside until flow is impeded. This happens first with the horizontal hot water lines, so check by starting outward from the water heater.

If the house has modernized kitchen and baths, it's likely that the whole plumbing system was updated when they were installed. If you're in doubt, ask.

If there is a well, you'll want proof of water quality and flow. If there is a septic system, ask questions about legal installation and past performance. (If sewers are available but not utilized, you may have trouble securing a mortgage loan.)

In some areas, buyers are understandably worried about a basement that might develop a running stream during spring thaws or summer storms. One quick way to judge is to see how much junk people store directly on a basement floor.

To see if a basement has flooded, inspect the bottom of the furnace and the water heater. Rust, or a newly painted neat strip across the bottom few inches, calls for an explanation. If a one-time flood occurred while the furnace was hot, there may be a cracked firebox.

Small amounts of damp on basement walls, though, are almost standard in some localities.

Pay little attention to the condition of the water heater. Even the most meticulous householder will use one down to the very end, so it isn't much of a clue to how the rest of the house has been maintained. And it is more of an appliance than a structural part of the house. Replacing it would not be a drastic enough expense to influence your decision on whether or not to buy.

☞ **Money-$aving Tip #23** *Look for plugged holes in the fascia or in the risers to the attic stairs, for spots where energy-saving insulation was blown in.*

The Condition of the Insulation

If an older house in a cold climate hasn't been adequately insulated, you will certainly do it yourself immediately. The best place for insulation is under the attic floor. Look for holes in the fascia or in the stair risers that were drilled for blown-in insulation and then plugged. Try to find out how many inches were installed. Some old jobs were very good indeed; others don't meet modern standards. Another simple installation with a fine payback is band insulation around the top of the basement wall, where the foundation meets the floor joists.

If a house in a northern state doesn't have good storm windows and screens, it probably doesn't have much else in terms of general modernization, for this is one of the first comfort items people buy. You don't need fancy metal self-storing ones. Properly fitting old-fashioned wooden storm windows can be even better than new metal ones, but are a bit of a hassle to put up and down.

If the house lacks insulation or storm windows, when you come to the time of the mortgage application, inquire about whether you may include the cost of energy-savers in your mortgage.

Don't pay a big premium just because the house has sidewall insulation. It's nice, of course, but it doesn't have the payback of that thick layer under the attic floor.

Environmental Hazards

The results are still out on the effect of electromagnetic radiation. Some early studies indicate increased rates of cancer in children who live close to high-voltage lines. Other studies show no effect on nearby residents at all. There's not yet any dependable guideline in this matter; emissions are easily tested, however.

☞ **Money-$aving Tip #24** *Radon problems in a home can be cured easily and inexpensively.*

One toxic substance you can't see for yourself is radon, a colorless odorless gas that seeps into houses from the earth itself. Testing can be unreliable unless carefully done; testing is done best by a professional. Simply using a test kit can yield false results if windows are kept open during the test, which takes several days. Some areas are at higher risk than others. Curing a radon problem is relatively simple and inexpensive, however, usually with specific ventilation in foundation and basement.

High levels of lead in children have been shown to affect mental and physical development. Lead paint is no longer used, but for most loans anyone considering a house built before 1978 must receive a written information sheet about it. Chipping paint is particularly dangerous. As with asbestos, removing lead paint can release dangerous amounts of the substance and should be done professionally. Sometimes the best solution is to cover it over. If it is to be removed, safety precautions must be taken.

Lead can also be found in drinking water. Simple tests can be done, preferably on early-morning samples. In an older home, it's wise to make a habit of starting your cooking with cold water; those pipes leach less lead than the hot-water ones. And you can run the water for a bit before using it first thing in the morning to get rid of lead that may have leached out during the night.

Asbestos was widely used before about 1975 in all sorts of building materials, from insulation to floor tiles. Its tiny fibers can cause lung cancer. Where it is intact and not deteriorating, it poses little or no danger. The most common problem may be heavy asbestos insulation wrapped around heat ducts leading from an old-fashioned furnace. Removing it releases the fibers; sometimes a problem is best solved by encasing the asbestos completely.

Professional Home Inspectors

First-time homebuyers often call in parents, uncles or best friends for advice on a home they're considering. Unfortunately, the amateur expert usually feels duty-bound to find something wrong with the property, and the buyer ends up even more confused. It's best to get your estimate of condition from a professional.

In many communities, home inspection services by a licensed engineer are available (see the yellow pages under

"Building Inspectors" or "Home Inspectors"). Those who ✳
belong to the American Society of Home Inspectors (ASHI) ✳✳
have met specific standards of education and experience. Ask
if the inspector does repair work or recommends contractors—and if the answer is "yes," look for another inspector.
You want someone who has nothing to gain by finding fault
with the property.

☞ **Money-$aving Tip #25** *Avoid home inspectors who
also do repair work or recommend contractors.*

You can hire an inspector before or after you make the
offer on the house; the next chapter has information on how
to make your purchase offer dependent upon a satisfactory
report. You may be charged a few hundred dollars, depending on travel time.

Try to accompany your inspector with a tape recorder.
You'll learn many interesting things about the house that
wouldn't be in a written report. The engineer can't tell you
what the house is worth or give you advice on whether to
buy it. Instead, you'll hear things like "That roof looks as if it
has another five years or so on it. If you had to replace it today,
it might cost..." Making the final decision is up to you.

Ask specifically whether there are indications that the
house needs a specialist's inspection for a toxic substance.

Visit Open Houses

Usually held on Saturday or Sunday afternoons, open
houses are an invitation to the general public to visit. You
won't need any advance appointment or research; you can
tour the areas that most interest you, stopping in at one house
after another. It's a great way to get a feeling for prices and
neighborhood conditions.

Don't hesitate to visit even if you're not ready to buy. Brokers can be lonely, giving up a Sunday afternoon to sit in a house, and will welcome you. Don't be worried if you're asked to sign in. If it were your house, wouldn't you want people to identify themselves before they came in? And of course you'll wipe your feet, restrain your children and put out your cigarette before entering.

Community practices differ in the matter of open-house etiquette among brokers. If you are working with one agent, discuss frankly the best way to visit open houses on your own when he or she isn't available. You don't want to find your dream house, only to find that you've stepped into jurisdictional disputes. Most agents can offer suggestions on how to head off such problems.

Finding the House Yourself

Of course, you'll read the real estate ads avidly while you are house-hunting. Particular real estate terms common to each area may puzzle you; don't hesitate to ask your agent to explain them. If you want to work through your own buyer's broker or through the one seller's agent who gives you good service, don't answer ads yourself. Phone your agent and mention the items that catch your eye, so that you'll have the advantage of professional handling of the initial contact with sellers. The broker can then do a little investigating, let you know if the property fits your wants and price range, and usually set up appointments to view.

How the Agent Can Help

House-hunting is of course the aspect of an agent's work that is most obvious to the public. The agent furnishes information to help you select the houses you want to view, sets up appointments, takes you through the properties and provides more detailed data on houses that particularly interest you.

Although they are not engineers, brokers can often alert you to obvious possible problems, and they are usually required to inform you of any hidden defects they are aware of. State law differs considerably, though, about intangible conditions that might bother one buyer and not another. In one state you must be informed about a murder on the property within the past three years; in another state a broker may not even answer questions about stigmatizing conditions like murder or suicide.

Real estate agents are familiar with local inspection services and can usually suggest several names for you to choose from. The agent can set up inspection appointments of all sorts as they are needed.

Commonly Asked Questions

Q. If we may be moving in a few years, what should we watch out for?

A. Find a house that will appeal to as many future buyers as possible. The easiest resale house is probably a fairly modern three-bedroom tract house in an area with a good school system.

Q. I've heard a great deal on cable TV about buying foreclosures. Is that a good way to find a bargain?

A. Yes, there are bargains to be had in foreclosures. What they don't tell you about on TV are the drawbacks.

Foreclosed property is sold at public auction. If you go, you may find the mortgage lender starting the bidding at the amount owed; the good part is that sometimes one dollar above that will take it.

One drawback is that you must buy for cash, or nearly so. Procedures vary in different areas. You must furnish immediately a certified check for perhaps 10 percent and might be offered something like a month to come up with the rest of the money. That may or may not be enough time to arrange a mortgage loan—and you or the property might not meet lender's standards for a loan in time.

Another problem is that the unfortunate owner need not let you in to inspect the property before you bid on it; you'll have to take your chances sight unseen. And many times people who couldn't pay their mortgage haven't been able to keep up with repairs either; the place may need some work.

If you do want to try for foreclosures, you'll find them advertised in at least one local newspaper. You can contact the law firm mentioned in the ad for details. It's best to have your own lawyer guiding you through the procedure, which varies from one locality to another.

Q. What about FHA and VA foreclosures?

A. Those are a bit different. The houses are already owned by the government, are vacant, and some of them are renovated. Mortgages are available if you qualify. The properties are usually described in local newspaper ads, with addresses, number of rooms and minimum bids listed. You can inspect the houses by contacting local brokers, who will have keys to open them. To make an offer, you work through regular real estate agencies, who forward the paperwork to the agency involved along with your earnest money deposit. Sealed bids are opened at the same time, and you will hear fairly promptly whether you are successful.

A house you buy in that fashion may well go under market value, but it won't be dirt-cheap in the fashion they promise on those get-rich-quick TV programs.

Q. Can I buy with nothing down?

A. Sometimes. For detailed information, see Chapter 9.

CHAPTER 8

Negotiating an Airtight Contract

You begin the process of arriving at a binding contract to purchase by giving the sellers your offer to buy, which includes not only price but many other provisions. The document is a written purchase offer; when the seller accepts it exactly as you presented it, it becomes a binding sales contract, which may be known in your community as a deposit receipt, contract of sale, or agreement to buy and sell.

All real estate contracts must be in writing in order to be enforceable. Nothing you and the seller say to each other is binding unless it's contained in the written document. If the sellers promise to leave the satellite dish, make sure the contract mentions it, or you could be out of luck.

☞ **Money-$aving Tip #26** *Never make an oral offer on a house. An acceptance wouldn't be binding, and you'd only reveal some of your buying strategy to the other party.*

Depending on local custom, a broker or attorney will usually help draw up the offer detailing the terms under which you propose to buy. In some areas this is a full-fledged contract, needing only the seller's acceptance to be complete. Elsewhere, local custom may employ a preliminary memorandum, articles of agreement, binder or deposit receipt.

It's foolish to try drawing up the offer for yourself. There's no use copying someone else's contract or a model; yours will differ in many respects according to the needs of the parties involved, local custom and state law. Brokers and lawyers must take courses, pass exams and gain related experience before they're allowed to fill out these forms. Don't try to do it yourself.

Ask the broker with whom you are working for a copy of the purchase offer that office uses, or obtain a copy of the contract generally used by your multiple-listing system or bar association. In some states a standard contract is mandated. Study the blank contract at leisure in advance, for when it comes time to fill one in and sign it, you'll be too nervous for quiet consideration.

Before you begin and before emotions take over, settle in your mind the top price you really would invest in the house— a figure you will not share with the agent, unless it is someone you specifically hired as your own broker. Keep that figure in mind during negotiations.

☞ **Money-Saving Tip #27** *Make up your mind in advance—and keep to yourself—how much you would really pay for the property if you had to.*

Hard-headed negotiators advise you not to fall in love with one particular property; remember there are others if you can't reach an agreement with this particular seller.

How Much To Offer

There's no set formula for whether you should offer less than the asking price. Homeowners who hate haggling may have listed their house at a rock-bottom price with no room for flexibility. Others may add a 5 percent cushion to what they'd really take.

The sellers' circumstances affect price. They may be under some of the pressures, such as foreclosure, mentioned in the last chapter. Elderly homeowners, on the other hand, are often in no hurry to move. They may have emotional ties that make it difficult for them to view their property impartially.

If a house has been on the market a long time (more than five months), the buying public has voted that it isn't worth what they're asking. In that case, don't offer full price.

☞ **Money-$aving Tip #28** *If a house has remained on the market for some time, it's probably not worth what the seller is asking.*

On the other hand, don't fool around if you've stumbled on a hot listing, one that has just come on the market and is uniquely appealing or is underpriced. If there is a possibility of several offers within the next day, consider coming in somewhere over the asking price. If you are already preapproved for a loan, include that information or accompany your offer with a financial statement. This gives you an advantage against competition. It may sound suspicious when a broker recommends such decisive action; this is where it helps if you already know and trust the agent.

Ask To See Comparables

When you house-hunt intensively in a given area, you quickly become an expert on homes that fall within your price range. You can recognize a bargain when it comes on the market. You can also spot overpriced property. For a short time, you may know more than anyone else in the world about the proper price for houses in a particular neighborhood.

In an unfamiliar area, ask the agent to show you sale prices of comparables ("comps"). These are similar homes in the neighborhood that have recently changed hands; they'll give you something to judge by. Comparables, in fact, are the principal tool brokers themselves use to appraise property for market value. Other considerations in making price comparisons include the condition of the house, time of year, special financing available and the general economic climate—whether it's a buyers' or sellers' market.

Remember that the seller's broker may furnish comps but is not supposed to suggest that you offer anything under the listed price for the house you are considering. If you have hired your own buyer's broker, you can expect advice on the lowest offer that might be accepted for the house.

The Owners' Cost Doesn't Count

You may be curious about what the homeowners paid three years ago for the place you want to buy today, but that is not relevant. The sellers' initial cost for the property shouldn't affect what you offer to pay for it. If they had received it as a gift, must they then give it away? Or, on the other hand, if they've invested $25,000 in a fancy swimming pool, are you then obliged to reimburse them? Of course not.

How much money the sellers have invested in the property and how much they need to get out of it are their concerns, not yours. In the end, runs the professional appraiser's maxim, "buyers make value." Selling price is set by the operation of supply and demand, in competition on the open market.

Don't pay much attention to the tax assessment on the property either. Even in communities that aim toward full-value assessment, the figures are seldom an accurate reflection of true value.

Your Situation Matters

Your offering price will be affected by the terms under which you expect to buy. If the sellers have to wait around while you market your present home, they'll be less inclined to drop their price. The same applies if they must come up with a cash payment of points to your lender. By the same token, a clean offer with no contingencies is worth a price concession. If you are already preapproved for a mortgage loan, that's particularly attractive to sellers.

☞ **Money-$aving Tip #29** *If you are preapproved for a loan, that may be useful in price negotiations.*

After price, the next big item in the contract is how you will finance your purchase. If you are going to assume a present loan or place your mortgage with the sellers themselves, these terms are detailed. You'll stipulate that the mortgage you are taking over must be current (paid up to date) at the time of transfer.

Provide for Contingencies

If you must obtain outside financing, the details of your proposed mortgage are spelled out, along with a statement that the contract is "contingent upon" or "subject to" your obtaining the loan. If you cannot find financing at the specific interest rate you have stipulated in the offer, you couldn't be required to go through with the purchase. The contract should state that in such a case your deposit would be returned.

There may be other contingencies (happenings) that must be satisfied before you will buy. You may need to sell your present home, obtain the job you came to town to interview for, or receive a satisfactory (to you) engineer's report. These conditions are written into the contract.

The sellers will be nervous about contingent offers. They will be taking their house off the market in your behalf, without any guarantee the sale will go through. So it's customary to set a time limit on contingencies. The contract might state that it is "contingent upon buyer's receiving a satisfactory engineer's report on the property within three days of acceptance of this offer" or "contingent upon approval by the buyer's husband when he arrives here next week."

For longer contingencies, particularly those involving the sale of your present house, the sellers may envision waiting around forever. Instead of worrying about the sale of their home, they must now worry about yours, over which they have even less control.

So it's only fair to insert an *escape clause,* or *kick-out.* The wording may differ according to local practice, but the escape clause usually gives the seller the right to continue to show the house. If another good offer comes in, you may be required to remove the contingency and make your offer firm or else drop out.

If your contingency is called, you don't have to meet anyone else's offering price; your deal has been nailed down. But you would have to agree, for example, to buy the property whether or not you sell your present home. Otherwise, you could drop out and receive your deposit back.

List Grey-Area Personal Property

It is essential to spell out in the contract all the grey-area items (carpeting, fireplace equipment, chandeliers, drapes) about which there may be disputes as to whether they stay with the property or not.

In general, personal property that can be picked up and moved without leaving any nail or screw holes may be taken by the seller. The rules are complicated, though, and it's best to stipulate in the contract that "stove and refrigerator are to remain" or "seller may remove antique dining-room chandelier."

Items like wall-to-wall carpeting, wood stoves, swing sets and satellite dishes are subject to occasional differences of opinion; head off trouble by detailing them in the written offer. If the listing agent did a proper job, the sellers will already have indicated which items they are taking or leaving. Ask the broker to do some delicate investigating about the sellers' plans for the above-ground pool or the tool shed.

Don't get bogged down over small items. Just make sure your offer specifies what you expect to remain. Don't discuss furniture or rugs you might like to buy at this point; wait until you have a firm purchase contract.

Your offer should stipulate that you have the right to inspect the premises within 24 hours of closing. You will want to make sure the sellers left the fireplace tools or removed the piles of magazines in the attic.

Also necessary in the contract are a target closing date and place for the actual transfer of title. Choose a date that will allow for processing of your mortgage application; the agent will have suggestions.

What if that date comes and goes? You still have a binding contract. If a certain deadline is absolutely essential, you can use the powerful legal phrase "time is of the essence" but this is strong medicine; don't do it without consulting your lawyer.

Experience has taught agents and lawyers to provide for all sorts of complications that may not have occurred to you. What if the house burns down before closing? If the bank's appraiser thinks it isn't worth the price you're paying? If taxes weren't paid last year? If the sellers can't prove they have clear title (ownership)? If there's a full tank of oil left in the basement? Will you receive occupancy on the day you settle? Will you receive a full warranty deed, or does local custom use a lesser deed? All these questions should be answered in a well-drawn contract.

Set a Time Limit

You will set a time limit on your offer, and it should be a short one. A day or two is enough time for the sellers to consider your proposal. If you give them more time, they may be tempted to stall until after they see what next Sunday's open house might bring. They might also use your offer as an auction goad to bid up another prospective buyer. If the sellers are out of town, they should be available by phone and could answer your offer by fax with a confirming letter to follow.

Earnest Money Deposit

An offer to buy is usually accompanied by a substantial deposit, variously known as binder or earnest money. This sum serves several purposes. It proves to the sellers that you mean business. They are, after all, going to take the place off the market on your behalf. The deposit also serves as a source of damages if you back out for no good reason a month down the line. The deposit is usually placed with a broker or attorney, who puts it into a separate escrow, or trust, account. Don't give the deposit directly to the seller, who may not understand the legal responsibility of holding some-one else's money, or the circumstances under which it must be returned to you.

You may be told that 6 percent or 10 percent of the purchase price is necessary. If this is inconvenient, insist that you can come up with only a smaller amount. Remember, though, that the sellers are weighing your offer to see if it will result in a successful sale. Without much earnest money, it may not look convincing.

This earnest money, of course, counts toward the sum you'll need at closing. It doesn't add to your costs. Your full deposit is credited toward the down payment or other settle-ment expenses. The contract should clearly state under what circumstances it may be returned.

Having a House Built

If you're buying a brand-new house or having one built, your contract should include a promise of a warranty for faults that may show up during the first year. The possibilities of negotiating on price with a builder or developer are limited; their price is based on cost and, except in hardship situations, is not usually too flexible. It may be possible, though, to dicker for extras that otherwise involve add-on prices.

Make sure the contract provides for proof that subcontrac-tors are paid before the closing, and try for a provision that some of the purchase price will be held in escrow after closing to insure prompt attention to problems that may surface soon after you move in.

Other Contract Provisions

✳   The contract provides that you will receive clear title, full unchallenged control and ownership, except for certain liens and easements that are spelled out. These are claims that third parties may have against the property. You agree to take it even though the telephone company has the right to run wires through the backyard, or the neighbor the right to

✳   share the driveway; these are known as easements of record. You don't agree to be responsible for unknown liens (financial claims) that turn up later, like an unpaid roofing bill or an outstanding home-improvement loan.

Remember that except where something illegal is involved, everything is negotiable. If some provisions on a standard preprinted contract are not acceptable to you, they can be crossed out (with the party who did so initialing the changes.) You can also insert anything that you particularly want in the contract. Of course, to make it binding you'll have to find a seller who accepts your changes.

If this is your first homebuying experience, you will feel shaky when time comes to sign the offer. You should receive an immediate duplicate of everything you sign; if duplicates aren't offered, ask for them. You need not walk out wondering what you've just committed yourself to.

Your Lawyer's Role

You can safely follow local custom about whether an attorney or agent writes an uncomplicated contract. It's reassuring to take the contract to your lawyer before you sign it. Many sales, though, are made after office hours and on weekends, and you may risk losing the right house by delay. You can write above your signature "subject to the approval in form of my attorney." This means that you can go ahead and make your offer, while reserving for your lawyer the right to object later to any wording or provisions that don't protect your interests. The lawyer can even disapprove the whole contract.

Most lawyers refuse to give advice on price, feeling this is out of their field of expertise. The attorney's job is to see that the contract protects you and accomplishes your objectives.

The Negotiation Process

Although local customs vary, in most areas the broker will present your offer to the seller. You'll be advised to go home and wait by the phone. The agent, meanwhile, may contact the listing broker and the seller, to arrange for presentation of the offer as soon as possible; prompt forwarding of all offers is one of the broker's primary legal responsibilities. Agents are required by law to present any written offer to the seller immediately. They may not refuse to present an offer no matter how small.

Federal fair housing laws mandate that your offer must be considered without reference to your race, color, country of origin, handicap, religion, gender or the presence of children in your family. Laws in your particular state may add other protected classes: age, for example, or lawful source of income.

The broker almost never reveals terms or price over the phone. The seller cannot accept over the phone and deserves the right to look over all the details of your proposal at leisure.

The next move is the seller's. The response can be "yes" (acceptance), "no" (refusal) or "maybe" (counteroffer). If it's yes, the seller accepts all your terms, and you have a binding contract. If it's no, the homeowners cannot later change their minds and accept your offer after all. You are no longer bound by that offer.

Rather than an outright refusal, though, a good negotiator will bring you a counteroffer: "We accept all terms and conditions except that purchase price shall be $183,000, and we'll include in that price the stove and refrigerator now in the first-floor kitchen."

The seller is now bound by the counteroffer, which probably contains a time limit, while you are free to consider its terms. If you are told that the agreement is firm if you'll just initial a couple of small changes, be aware than you are not bound and can drop out. Any change the seller has made in your offer constitutes a counteroffer, and you needn't initial those changes unless you feel like accepting them.

You may want to counter a price counteroffer, perhaps split the difference. Too many back-and-forths, though, result in hard feelings and often kill the deal. People begin to say, "It's not the money, it's the principle of the thing." Instead of working together toward what is legally known as a meeting of the minds, buyer and seller start to see the negotiation as a war. They concentrate on winning and lose sight of their original goals. If negotiations become protracted, try not to let personal feelings affect your decisions. Never insult the other party.

Before you start, make up your mind that you will not lose the house you really want over the last thousand dollars. When you cannot make any further concessions on price, try to include a deal-saving gesture toward the seller. If you're not willing to go higher on price, perhaps you can change the closing date for the seller's convenience. Make your first offer, certainly your second one, close to the top price you'd really pay. The idea is to tempt the sellers to wrap up the deal, even if it isn't quite what they had in mind.

Who Is Bound by the Offer

At each stage, the person who made the last proposal is bound by it until it's withdrawn or answered. The process ends when one side accepts unconditionally the other's last offer—or drops out. Remember that if your proposal is accepted, you will have a binding legal contract. Don't fool around with a purchase offer unless you really want to buy the property.

How *the Agent Can Help*

An agent can furnish you with comparable sales figures on nearby property. A buyer's broker can go further and recommend an offering price based on those comparable sales and also on what is known about the seller's situation.

In most areas, either a seller's or a buyer's broker can fill out the blanks in a preprinted standard purchase contract.

If you belong to a class of people protected under fair housing law, the agent can and should remind sellers of your right to equal consideration with other buyers.

Bringing you and the seller into agreement is one of any agent's most skilled services. Ideally, each party comes away satisfied with the outcome, in a win/win situation. The agent is particularly valuable in serving as a buffer between you and the seller during what is usually a nervous time for both.

Referrals from satisfied clients and customers are an agent's most gratifying source of future business. Ideally, the broker hopes to demonstrate professionalism that earns your respect so that some day when real estate help is needed, you'll call again—or tell your friends to call again.

Commonly Asked Questions

Q. *Isn't the dining-room chandelier considered part of the real estate?*

A. Yes, but if it's a particularly desirable one, you'd be prudent to specify it in your purchase contract anyway, just to avoid annoying misunderstandings later.

Q. *Under what circumstances would our earnest money deposit be returned?*

A. That depends on the provisions in your contract. It usually states that you will receive your deposit back if you can't obtain the financing you had stipulated, if other contingencies aren't met or, in general, if the sale fails to go through for any reason that is not your fault.

Q. *The sellers told us they'd accept our offer if we "reduced it to writing." We did, but before we got it back to them they sold to someone else, and for less. Do we have a case against them?*

A. Probably not. No oral acceptance is binding. Until they signed something, they were free to deal with anyone they pleased. Although the price was lower, there may have been something they preferred about the other offer—the buyers' financial qualifications, perhaps. Your only just complaint would be if you suspected the rejection was a violation of fair housing law based on your membership in a protected group.

CHAPTER 9

Finding Financing for Your Future Home

Perhaps you plan to pay all cash for your home. Perhaps the seller has agreed to finance your purchase (take back a mortgage for part of the sale price). Perhaps you have already obtained mortgage preapproval from a lending institution.

But if you are like most homebuyers, your next step after arriving at a firm purchase contract is to apply for a mortgage loan (in some states, a deed of trust is used instead of a mortgage, but it serves the same purpose).

Loan application is described in the next chapter, but before you start the financing process, it's wise to learn as much as you can about the mortgage market and the choices available to you.

There is no one best type of mortgage. More than 100 mortgage plans are probably available right now in your area, and each one is out there because it fits the needs of a particular buyer, seller or parcel of real estate.

For most buyers, the first place for guidance is an agent, either their own or a seller's. Within the first few minutes of conversation, any good agent begins, almost unconsciously, to plan a strategy for financing your loan. Those impertinent questions about your salary, cash on hand and present debts are important in helping you find the right way to manage your purchase.

Mortgage brokers, who bring borrowers and lenders together, can also be helpful, particularly if you are buying unusual property or have less-than-perfect qualifications. Look for a mortgage broker who is paid by you, not the lending institution chosen, and is paid only after the loan is secured.

☞ **Money-$aving Tip #30** *Look for a mortgage broker who is paid only after you receive a loan commitment.*

Prequalifying Versus Preapproval

Keep in mind the difference between prequalifying and preapproval. With the first, the lending institution gives you the same sort of estimate about what you could borrow that a real estate agent has probably already furnished.

With actual preapproval, however, the lender has verified your qualifications and furnished you with a definite commitment to lend you a certain sum, assuming the property you want to purchase passes the appraisal process.

Buying for All Cash

A purchase for all cash is, of course, the simplest and quickest method. It is also the most welcome to a seller and, in a normal open market sale, should be worth a concession on price.

You may run into an unusual situation that calls for immediate action—seller facing foreclosure, for example. Sometimes when there is a divorce or death in a family, owners are ready to accept a bargain price in return for quick cash.

If you do buy for all cash, you need to be extra-careful. When you must act quickly, resist the temptation to act without legal advice. You may need to sign an immediate purchase offer promising prompt settlement, but your own lawyer should insure that the offer protects you properly.

Without the protection of a mortgage lender's investigation, you need assurance that you are receiving clear, trouble-free title, that taxes are paid to date, that the seller has the right to transfer the property to you, that you aren't taking over old financial claims along with the real estate.

In some all-cash situations, the buyer must accept the physical condition of the property "as is." You may want to bring in a building inspection engineer before your purchase contract becomes firm so that you know what you are getting into.

Buying with No Down Payment

Can you really buy real estate with nothing down as promised on cable TV? Yes, you can. There are several ways, and they're no secret. You don't need to send away for books and tapes. Any good real estate broker knows the techniques and can tell you whether a particular plan fits your circumstances.

☞ **Money-$aving Tip #31** *Don't send away for costly courses on how to buy real estate. Local brokers will give you the same information for free.*

Veterans can place VA loans with nothing down and do it on houses valued at more than $200,000, if they qualify to carry the payments. If the seller agreed, a VA loan could even be placed with the seller furnishing all the buyer's closing costs.

For those with moderate income who want to live in rural areas, the Farmers Home Administration (Rural Economic and Community Development Administration) makes no-down-payment loans on modest properties, discussed further in this chapter. Monthly payments with Farmers Home can reflect mortgage interest rates as low as 1 percent, depending on family income.

Particularly with income property where the owner doesn't need to get the money out right away, you can always look for a seller who will turn the property over to you and finance your purchase, take back a mortgage, and if you look really good, perhaps do it with nothing down.

Although they're not available with nothing down, many other mortgage plans require a minimum of only 5 percent down and FHA loans a bit less than that.

Types of Mortgage Loans

Remember always that the lending institution is not doing you a favor. They're in business to lend money, and if you're qualified, they want you as a customer.

For the usual purchase, a smorgasbord of mortgage types is spread out for your consideration. At any time, perhaps 100 different plans will be available in the typical community. Dozens of terms describe particular mortgages: FHA, VA, assumable, purchase-money, second, package, balloon, portfolio, conventional, PMI, convertible, ARM. An agent contemplates this dazzling array, trying to fit your needs with current offerings.

Picking the right loan involves taking into consideration many factors beyond the quoted rate of interest: proposed down payment, your income and future prospects and plans, the seller's finances, current trends in interest rates, type and condition of the property, costs and fees.

When you're offered a loan at a particularly favorable rate, inquire about closing costs. Certain costs are standard: points, appraisal of the property, credit check on yourself, other legitimate charges. But some lenders inflate their profit with fake junk fees or garbage fees that might be listed as underwriting, document processing, document transfer, submission, commitment fees or the like. Depending on how much the lender wants your business, you could try negotiating about these nuisance charges. While you may not know the details about how lenders classify borrowers, if you represent a solid well-qualified Class A loan, you may have some bargaining power.

☞ **Money-$aving Tip #32** *If you're well-qualified, you may be able to negotiate away certain "garbage" fees.*

In some states, including California, a slightly different legal system uses a deed of trust instead of a mortgage. If your state is one of these, for practical purposes you can consider *deed of trust* and *mortgage* as interchangeable terms.

The Secondary Mortgage Market

Most mortgages, these days, are bundled into large packages and sold to big investors in what is known as the secondary market. Among the buyers are large insurance companies, banks and pension funds and, most important, organizations specifically set up to warehouse mortgages, like the Federal National Mortgage Association (Fannie Mae).

You may not always be notified if your mortgage is sold. Sometimes the original lender retains the servicing, collecting payments, handling paperwork and forwarding the money to the new holder of the mortgage.

In other cases, particularly when the buyer of the packaged mortgages is another bank, borrowers may be instructed to send their payments directly to the new mortgagee. Many borrowers feel betrayed when they find they are dealing with out-of-state institutions instead of their friendly local bank, but the system allows lenders to recoup their investment immediately and to channel more mortgage money back into the community.

When Fannie Mae, which owns perhaps 1 mortgage in 20 in this country, announces that it will buy packages of certain types of loan, lenders around the country quickly bring their mortgage plans into compliance. Other national standards are set by the Government National Mortgage Association (Ginnie Mae) and the Federal Home Loan Mortgage Corporation (Freddie Mac).

All of this can have an effect on your search for the perfect mortgage. When you find that most institutional lenders have identical top limits on the amount they'll lend, or analyze your income in the same way, that means they are probably planning to package your loan and sell it and are conforming to the requirements of the secondary market.

Portfolio Loans

In looking for the right mortgage plan, it helps to understand the difference between portfolio loans and those intended for the secondary market. If you have unusual qualifications, or unique property that doesn't fit usual standards, look for a portfolio or nonconforming loan.

Years ago, banks took part of their depositors' savings, lent it out on mortgages, collected monthly payments and, when enough money was returned, made more loans. This procedure is the exception these days. The bank that uses such a system is said to be making *portfolio* or nonconforming loans, keeping the mortgages as assets in its own portfolio.

If you have an unusual situation (for example, complicated self-employment income, the desire to pay your own property taxes and insurance instead of through the lender's escrow account, or a 200-year-old house that doesn't meet today's standards), find out which local lenders are currently making portfolio loans. With portfolio loans, lenders can be more flexible, making exceptions to their usual rules, subject only to state laws and their own judgment. Portfolio loans are sometimes called nonconforming, because they are not tailored to the requirements of the secondary market, or jumbo loans if they are for larger amounts than the secondary market will buy.

Where To Find a Lender

Don't be surprised if your lender turns out to be something different from the traditional "bank"—savings bank, commercial bank or savings and loan institution. While those entities are still very much in the mortgage business, there are new players.

Mortgage bankers (mortgage companies) are in business solely to make (originate) mortgage loans and handle the ensuing monthly paperwork (servicing). Unlike traditional banks, they take no depositors' savings and offer no checking accounts. They are active in the secondary market, selling packages of mortgages and turning the proceeds back into the community to make more loans. Mortgage banking firms have become a large part of the lending scene in the past decade.

Credit unions are often overlooked in the search for the right lender. If you belong to one, mention this fact to the broker with whom you are working and investigate for yourself whether your credit union offers mortgage loans. In some instances, favorable terms are available. For smaller mortgage loans that other lending institutions won't bother with, a credit union may be a good resource.

Mortgage brokers make no loans at all. Their role is to bring borrowers and lenders together. If you have an unusual situation or special needs, they can be particularly useful, because they may keep current with the offerings of many different lenders. Think twice, though, about paying a commission upfront, before a loan commitment is secured. Not all mortgage brokers require that.

Points about Points

Each point is 1 percent of a new loan being placed. If you buy a house for $150,000 and borrow $120,000, one point would equal $1,200 (not $1,500). Two points would be $2,400.

Points are charged by lending institutions as extra upfront, one-time lump-sum interest, when a new loan is placed.

They are usually paid at final settlement when the loan is actually made or, occasionally, at the time of mortgage application (in which case, find out whether they are refundable if the loan does not go through).

Sometimes you can pay extra points in return for special favors—a "lock-in" that guarantees you'll receive the rate in effect when you apply for the loan, no matter what has happened to rates in the meantime. But what if rates go down before your closing? Or you may be charged extra for an extension, if you don't close within a given period after the bank commits to making the loan.

When rates are fluctuating rapidly, some borrowers have been known to make mortgage application at two different lenders: one with rate locked in and one without. For whichever loan isn't eventually chosen, the wheeler-dealer will forfeit an application fee, usually several hundred dollars to cover at the least an appraisal and credit report. If widespread, the practice would pose a great nuisance to lenders, but it could give the applicant a chance to choose the more favorable loan at the last minute.

During negotiation of a sales contract, the seller will sometimes agree to pay the buyer's points, simply to expedite the sale. This can be particularly useful if the buyer is short on cash for closing.

Points paid by you as the buyer of your own residence are income tax deductible as interest, in the year they are paid. Points you pay to purchase income property must be amortized (deducted bit by bit over the years) along with other costs of placing an investor's loan.

Points paid by the seller are one of the expenses of selling and reduce the seller's capital gain on the sale. The buyer, however, is allowed to take points paid by either party as income tax deduction for interest expense for that year.

☞ **Money-$aving Tip #33** *You can deduct on that year's tax return points paid by either party on the purchase of your own main residence.*

Annual Percentage Rate (APR)

Which is better, a 9 percent, fixed-rate loan for 30 years with payment of 1 point plus a half-percent origination fee, or an adjustable-rate mortgage for 20 years, currently at 6 percent, with 4 points up front?

It's like comparing apples and oranges. First, of course, you must decide whether you have a gambler's instinct and will enjoy following interest rates and taking a chance on future payments being higher or lower. If rates are currently at the lower end of their inevitable cycle, you might prefer a fixed-rate loan. But trying to compare rates on such different mortgage plans, with varying closing costs, is like working with those apples and oranges.

To aid the consumer, lenders are required to quote you an annual percentage rate (APR), which takes into account points and certain closing costs. Suppose you do pay 6 percent, but with 4 extra points in a lump sum at closing. Clearly, your rate is really more than 6 percent. It's not 6 plus 4, because you pay those 4 points only once, not every year. But it's more than 6. How much more? That's the APR. Not all lenders calculate it in the same fashion, but it is useful for comparison shopping.

Conventional Mortgages

Loans agreed upon between you and the lender, without any government intervention except for overall banking regulations, are known as conventional mortgages. Because banking theory holds that it is unsafe to lend more than 80 percent of the value of the property, the standard conventional loan requires 20 percent down. With a 20 percent down payment, you have an 80 percent loan-to-value ratio (LVR).

If you are putting less than 20 percent down on a conventional loan, you will be asked to carry private mortgage insurance (PMI). This insurance, for which you pay a small premium, has nothing to do with life or health insurance. Instead, it protects the lending institution in case the loan goes sour and the property can't be sold for enough to cover the debt. Because this lowers the lender's risk, you can sometimes borrow with as little as 5 percent down (95 percent LVR).

Adjustable-Rate Mortgages

Until the early 1980s, almost all mortgages were fixed-rate, with the borrower knowing in advance exactly what the monthly payment would run for principal and interest over the full 25 or 30 years of a loan.

As interest rates began to skyrocket and finally hit 18 percent, lenders found themselves locked into unprofitable long-term commitments to keep their money lent out at rates like 5, 6 and 7 percent. This led to serious problems for lending institutions, and many were reluctant to make any further fixed-interest loans.

What emerged was the adjustable-rate mortgage, the ARM. The ARM shifts the risk of changing interest rates to the borrower, who also stands to benefit if rates drop during the period of the loan. It is often chosen when interest rates are high; when rates drop, most borrowers prefer to lock in fixed-rate loans. Those who plan to remain in a house for only a short time may opt for an adjustable rate that starts low and won't be adjusted for three, five or even seven years.

☞ **Money-$aving Tip #34** *Consider an adjustable-rate mortgage when interest rates are high.*

To choose wisely, the borrower must shop around, asking about the details of each ARM loan to find the one best suited to his or her own situation. And judging adjustable-rate mortgages requires understanding a whole new vocabulary.

The interest rate on your loan may go up or down, according to an *index* that follows the trend for interest rates across the country. To keep things fair, your lender must key the changes to some national indicator of current rates. It must be outside the control of your lender, and it should be a figure you can check for yourself, as published in the business sections of newspapers.

The most commonly chosen index is the rate at which investors will currently lend money to the government through purchase of United States Treasury notes or bills. The index used for your ARM loan might be the rate on sales of one-year, three-year, or five-year Treasury obligations (e.g., "one-year T-bills . . .").

Another index might be the average mortgage interest rate across the country for the preceding six months (Federal Home Loan Bank Board Cost of Funds). This index changes more slowly than, for example, the one-year T-bill. It could work for or against you, depending on the general direction of rates.

If Treasury bills are the chosen index, and they are selling at 6 percent interest, your lender will not make mortgage loans at that rate. Rather, you will pay a specific percentage, a *margin,* above the index.

If you are offered a 2 percent margin, you would pay 8 percent. If at the time of interest adjustment, Treasury bills had gone to 7 percent, a 2 percent margin would set your mortgage rate at 9 percent. If they had dropped to 5.5 percent, your interest would drop to 7.5 percent.

The word *cap* is used in two ways. First, your loan agreement may set, for example, a 2 percent cap on any upward adjustment. If interest rates (as reflected by your index) had gone up 3 percent by the time of adjustment, your rate could be raised only 2 percent.

When choosing an ARM, ask what happens in the above example. Is the extra 1 percent saved to be used for "catch-up" at the next adjustment, even though interest rates might have remained level? Or will you have negative amortization (see below)?

A *ceiling* (sometimes also called a lifetime cap) is an interest rate beyond which your loan can never go. Typically, you may be offered a 5-point ceiling. This means that if your loan starts at 8 percent, it can never go beyond 13 percent, no matter what happens to national interest rates. A ceiling allows you to calculate your *worst case*.

If your 30-year adjustable loan for $85,000 now costs $510 a month for principal and interest at 6 percent, and if your ceiling is 5 percent, the worst that could ever happen is that your interest rate would go to 11 percent. You can and should calculate in advance what that could cost you—$809 a month.

Regular amortization involves the gradual paying down of the principal borrowed, through part of your monthly payments. If, however, your monthly payments aren't enough to cover even the interest due, *negative amortization* is a possibility.

Suppose that interest on your loan should total $700 a month. For some reason, however, your monthly payment is set at $650. The shortfall, $50 a month, may be added to the amount you have borrowed. At the end of the year you'd owe not less, but about $600 more, than when you started.

Negative amortization could result from an artificially low initial interest rate, or it could follow a hike in rates larger than your cap allows the lender to impose. Not all mortgage plans include the possibility of negative amortization. Sometimes the lender agrees to absorb any shortfalls. But you should ask if it is a possibility, and in what fashion, before choosing a specific ARM.

☞ **Money-$aving Tip #35** *Always ask if an ARM might involve negative amortization.*

Different ARM plans may or may not set a cap on *decreases* in your rate, either at each adjustment period, or over the whole life of the loan. With a floor, you could calculate the best case for your loan—your lowest possible payment if interest fell deeply during the life of the loan.

If your mortgage offers *convertibility,* you may have the best of both worlds. You can choose to convert your adjustable-rate mortgage to a fixed-rate loan if you'd like.

With some plans, you can seize any favorable time (when fixed rates are generally low) during the life of the mortgage; more commonly, you can make the choice on certain anniversaries of the loan. Cash outlay for the conversion is low compared with the costs of placing a completely new mortgage; 1 point, or 1 percent of the loan, is typical. Be sure to inquire what it would be.

You may, however, pay a slightly higher interest rate all along, in return for the option. And be sure you understand what rate you'd be able to convert to. Often it too is slightly higher than whatever the lender is offering at that time. Keep in mind that if interest rates ever dropped sharply, you could always pay off your present loan and simply refinance to a new one.

With most ARM loans, during the first year, or the first adjustment period, the rate is set artificially low to induce the borrower to enter into the agreement—a "teaser" or "come-on" rate. Buyers who plan to be in a house for only a few years may be delighted with such arrangements, especially if no interest adjustment is planned for some years. Other borrowers, however, may end up with negative amortization and payment shock.

The prudent borrower asks, "If you were not offering this initially lower rate, what would my true interest be today? If things remained exactly the same, what rate (and what dollar amount) would I be paying after the first adjustment period?"

The borrower who starts out with an artificially low rate may easily carry the payments. Suppose, however, that the rate eventually rises to the full ceiling allowed. Result: a bad attack of *payment shock,* leading in some cases to foreclosure and loss of the property. After many bad experiences, most lenders require borrowers to qualify to carry the payments at next year's rate, even if this year's is low.

☞ **Money-$aving Tip #36** *Ignore low initial interest rates on an adjustable-rate mortgage and ask instead what the current rate should be.*

Your *adjustment period* is the length of time between interest rate adjustments. Typically made at the end of each year, adjustments might also be made as often as every six months or as infrequently as every seven years. With some loans, interest rates may be adjusted although monthly payments are not. This could result in negative amortization or, if rates had gone down while payments didn't, in faster reduction of the principal owed.

Extra, upfront, lump-sum payment of interest may bring down the interest rate charged on a loan. In some cases, the lower rate lasts for the whole life of the loan. In a 3-2-1 *buydown,* however, interest is reduced 3 percent for the first year of the loan, 2 percent the next year, 1 percent the third year. After that, interest reaches normal levels. Any plan offering a lower interest rate in return for more upfront points is, in effect, a buydown.

Length of the Loan

Thirty-year mortgage loans have been losing some popularity to 20-year and even 15-year mortgages. Monthly payments on a 15-year loan can run about 20 percent higher than on the same loan figured on a 30-year basis. You would need about 20 percent more income to qualify for the shorter loan. On the other hand, you'd make payments only half as long and cut your total interest cost considerably.

The 15-year mortgage operates like enforced saving, because it requires you to pay off the debt faster. It may be appropriate if, for example, your children will be starting college in 15 years, at a time when you'd like to own your house free and clear.

☞ **Money-$aving Tip #37** *Always check your annual statement to make sure extra principal payments were properly credited. Lending institutions can make mistakes too.*

It does tie up your money, however. If you have the discipline, there's nothing to stop you from putting that extra money, each month, into your own savings account, where you can tap it as needed and where it will earn extra interest.

FHA Mortgages

The Federal Housing Authority (FHA), an agency of the Department of Housing and Urban Development (HUD), was established to help homeowners buy with low down payments. Lenders can safely make loans of up to 97 percent of the value of property, because the FHA insures them against loss in case of foreclosure.

If FHA loans are used in your area, they can be a fine way to go. The money comes not from the government but from local lenders, so if none in your locality is handling FHA mortgages, you're out of luck. The loans are not intended for expensive property, but upper limits in high-price areas are raised from time to time. In the mid-1990s, the maximum FHA loan was $151,725; in low-cost counties it was $77,197.

For inexpensive property (under $50,000), down payment can be as low as 3 percent; in any case it runs less than 5 percent. FHA loans may be placed on one-family to four-family dwellings and are intended for owner-occupants.

FHA insurance premiums (to protect the lender in case of default) are due in a lump sum at closing and can run up to 2.25 percent of the loan. Because most FHA buyers don't have extra cash at closing, the mortgage insurance premium (MIP) can be added to the amount of the mortgage loan. If you pay off your FHA mortgage within the first few years, a portion of your MIP is returned. In addition to the one-time MIP, you'll pay one-half percent of the outstanding balance each year. The number of years this extra premium is charged depends on the size of the down payment; minimum-down loans require the extra charge over the longest period.

In addition to the standard FHA program, #203-b, others are available in certain areas. FHA 203-k, for example, lends money to cover both the cost of a home in need of substantial rehabilitation and the money needed for repairs.

Your real estate broker will know whether any or all of these programs are available in your community—or you can sit down with the yellow pages open to "Mortgages" and spend a couple of hours calling around yourself. If FHA is not handled locally, you can talk with a mortgage broker about whether your mortgage could be placed elsewhere.

The outstanding feature that has made FHA loans particularly desirable in the past is their assumability by the person to whom you might sell your property in the future. New regulations, however, limit this advantage; see the discussion on assumability below.

VA (GI) Mortgages

The most attractive thing about VA loans is the possibility of no down payment. In addition, a cooperative seller (if you can locate one) is allowed to furnish some or all of your closing costs and even furnish some of the prepaid taxes and insurance required at closing; you could conceivably buy without using a cent of your own money. There is, however, no subsidy involved, and you must qualify to carry the payments as you would with any other mortgage. VA loans may be used for one-family to four-family houses, owner-occupied only. They are assumable (with the restrictions listed below in the discussion of assumptions).

As with FHA mortgages, the money comes from a local lender; the Department of Veterans Affairs' contribution is to guarantee the loan at no cost to the veteran. While FHA loans require low down payments, VA loans may be made for the entire appraised value of the property (100 percent LVR). In the mid-1990s, the VA would guarantee loans as high as $203,100.

VA Qualifications

For a VA-guaranteed loan, the veteran needs a discharge "other than dishonorable" and either 180 days' active (not reserve) duty between September 16, 1940, and September 7, 1980, or 90 days' service during a war (the Korean, Viet Nam and Gulf conflicts are considered wars). Two years of active service after September 7, 1980, also qualifies, as does six years of service in the Reserve or National Guard. In-service VA mortgages are also possible.

Eligibility for such mortgages does not expire. If one's first VA loan is paid off, full eligibility is regained. At closing, a funding fee is paid directly to the Department of Veterans Affairs.

Subsidized Payments

In rural areas, direct mortgage loans can sometimes be obtained from the Farmers Home Administration (FmHA, Rural Economic and Development Administration, Department of Agriculture). If your income falls within specific limits (fairly low, depending on family size) you can buy a modest home on no more than one acre, with interest payments tailored to your income.

The program is intended for those who cannot obtain financing elsewhere. The money is allotted to local offices quarterly. At any given time, some offices will have money available; others will have waiting lists. The FmHA processes mortgage applications before you've found a house, then notifies you as money becomes available.

From time to time, various other programs are offered by states or municipalities, to build up their housing stock or to help first-time buyers get into the market. It's always worth calling your town or city hall to inquire whether there's something offered that would be of value to you. Brokers usually stay informed on local programs and on the loans offered through most of the states.

The National Council of State Housing Agencies, at 202-624-7710, can give you a phone number for your state's office.

Assumable Mortgages

If you may have trouble qualifying for a new loan, have your agent search for houses with freely assumable mortgages. An assumable mortgage is one that can remain with the property when it is sold. This results in considerable savings for the next buyer; no outlay for the costs associated with placing a new mortgage–items like appraisal of the property, mortgage tax, etc. A high assumable mortgage, or one at a low interest rate, is therefore worth a premium and contributes extra value to property on the market.

FHA loans made before December 1, 1986, and VA loans made before March 1, 1988 are completely, "freely," assumable. This means that you, or anyone else the seller chooses, can take the loan along with the real estate, just as it stands. Neither you nor the house need pass any evaluation by the lending institution, which has no say in the matter. Closing costs are negligible, the interest rate will not change and the transaction can be closed, settled, as soon as the parties wish.

In areas where prices have risen, of course, these older loans represent only part of the value of the property. You must pay the seller the rest of the purchase price in cash, unless you can persuade the owner to take back financing. The seller who does that agrees to hold a second mortgage for part of the purchase price, or even–in rare instances–for the entire missing amount (nothing down!).

You'd have to look pretty good financially before a seller would enter into such an arrangement, because even though you take over the payments on the loan and ownership of the property, the seller retains liability for that FHA or VA debt if anything goes wrong.

Assumable with Approval

Newer FHA and VA loans are classified as "assumable with bank approval." To take over a newer FHA mortgage, you must prove qualification (income and credit) to the lending institution's satisfaction. Once that's done, if you make the payments promptly the original borrower retains liability for only five years. With new VA mortgages, the person assuming the loan (who need not be a veteran) must qualify with the lender before any assumption. A charge of no more than $500 may be made for the paperwork.

Besides FHA and VAs, many adjustable-rate mortgages have assumability features, which allow for considerable savings on closing costs. ARM mortgages differ; most stipulate that the new borrower must qualify with the lender and that the interest rate may be adjusted upon assumption. Some charge is made for the privilege; 1 point might be typical.

Other Sources for Mortgage Money

A seller may agree to hold financing, lending you money on a first mortgage or, if the property already has one, on a second (typically shorter-term) loan. A family member may agree to lend you part of the purchase price, in which case it is prudent to keep things on a business-like basis, offering the property as security for a regular mortgage. Doing so will also allow you an income-tax deduction for interest paid; if the property is not pledged, you'd be paying nondeductible interest on a simple personal loan.

Family members may offer low-interest or no-interest loans, but the Internal Revenue Service takes a dim view of them. It likes to see a private mortgage loan made at either 9 percent or the "applicable federal rate," an index published monthly by the government, which follows current trends in interest rates. If the mortgage rate does not meet that standard, the IRS will *impute* the interest and tax the lender as if it had been received anyhow.

Land Contracts and Lease-Options

A *land contract* (contract for deed, contract sale) is a type of layaway installment plan for buying a house. Typically it is sought by a buyer who does not have enough down payment to qualify for a bank loan or to persuade the seller to turn over title (ownership). You move in, make monthly payments to the seller and take care of taxes, insurance and repairs exactly as if you owned the place. But title does not transfer to you until a specified time, perhaps when you make the final payment. With some land contracts, you receive title when you have made enough payments to constitute 20 percent equity. *Equity* is defined as the amount you "have in" the property—roughly, market value minus debt owed. Often the expectation is that you will qualify for a regular mortgage loan along the way, and pay off the land contract.

A *lease-option* differs from a land contract in that you are not bound to buy the property. Instead, you move in as a tenant and typically pay a flat amount, perhaps $1,000 or $2,000, in return for an option—the right to purchase at a given price within a given time (typically one, two or three years) if you so choose. If you decide not to buy, you simply remain as a tenant for the duration of the lease. Who pays for what expenses and whether any of your rent goes toward the purchase price are negotiable items.

Any land contract or lease-option requires extra-careful consultation with your own attorney before you sign anything. Such contracts can vary considerably in their provisions, and you must have someone on your side making sure your interests are protected. Either type of contract should be recorded—entered in the public records to notify the world at large of your rights in the property.

Balloon Mortgages

Before agreeing to a balloon mortgage, it's essential to understand exactly how it works. Suppose an 80-year-old seller is ready to take back a $100,000 mortgage on the house you are buying from him. That means he'd act as the bank and lend you the money to purchase. It might be because the house could not meet bank standards and he is unable to do the necessary repairs; it could be because he'd prefer regular monthly income to realizing a lump sum; it could be because you have unusual circumstances (just starting your own business) that don't let you qualify for a bank loan.

At age 80, however, the seller will be comfortable only if he can count on seeing all his money within ten years. But if you pay at the proper rate for a 10-year loan your monthly payments will be more than you can handle. So you offer the seller a *balloon* mortgage. Your payments will be calculated, principal and interest, as if you were paying on a 30-year schedule. But at the end of ten years, whatever you still owe will be immediately all due and payable.

Because during the early years of a loan most of the monthly payment goes for interest, you will not reduce the principal much over those ten years. You will still owe about 90 percent of the original loan. That final balloon payment will be a big one. A five-year balloon mortgage is sometimes referred to as "60 and surprise"—the surprise being that big 61st payment.

☞ **Money-$aving Tip #38** *If you are using a balloon mortgage, be sure you have some good plan for refinancing when the balloon goes up.*

The usual understanding is that your finances will have straightened out, you will have built up equity (the money you've paid off plus any increase in value), the house will have been repaired and you can place a mortgage with a regular lending institution at that point. Or the old gentleman may still be in good health and so dependent on your prompt and regular checks that he agrees to renew the loan.

Financing New Construction

Financing new construction is easiest if you are working with a large builder, who may provide the money or help you arrange a building loan that later converts to a mortgage. If you are buying your own building lot, you will find banks reluctant to lend on vacant land. You'll have to buy for cash or persuade the seller to hold a mortgage.

Once the land is paid for, you can count it toward equity to help qualify for another loan. Building loans are most readily obtained after you have taken all the necessary steps to have your plans and lot approved by local authorities, and if you are working through a recognized contractor. Do-it-yourselfers, particularly those building on a shoestring, find it very difficult to obtain financing.

How *the Agent Can Help*

An agent's services start with that first interview, at which time you are given a rough idea of how much you could borrow on a mortgage loan or (in some states) a trust deed.

Keeping up with the constantly shifting local mortgage market is one of the real estate broker's most time-consuming tasks. Any good broker will advise on which mortgage plans seem most appropriate for your particular transaction. As you search for the best mortgage plan, the agent can also advise on which local lenders are most efficient.

In many communities, it's customary for the agent to make an appointment for your mortgage application and accompany you to the interview. Many lenders are also willing to come to your broker's office, or even to your home if necessary.

Commonly Asked Questions

Q. How do I find the best lender?

A. It doesn't make much difference what institution originates your mortgage loan, as long as it has a reputation for fairly efficient paperwork. Particularly if it merely originates loans for sale to the secondary market, you needn't be concerned once you receive the check. Concentrate instead on shopping for the best *loan,* considering interest rate, closing costs and other fees.

Q. Is it a good idea to take a larger mortgage for the tax deduction benefits?

A. It never makes sense to borrow money and pay interest just to get an income tax deduction. If you can choose whether to make a large down payment or a small one, whether to borrow more or less, make your decision based on your total financial situation, your age, how long you plan to stay in the house and similar factors. Ignore the tax aspects of the choice.

From a tax point of view, paying off a mortgage early is the same sort of choice, because the money you use to pay it off could otherwise be earning taxable interest elsewhere. Make your decision on how large a mortgage and how fast a payoff fit your particular needs. Income tax considerations should not enter into that particular decision.

Q. If we buy with an FHA mortgage and a defect turns up that was missed by their inspector, can we sue the FHA?

A. If the FHA inspector happens to miss anything, you have no recourse against the FHA or HUD. The same applies to VA loans. You agree to this when you apply for one of those loans.

CHAPTER 10

Securing Quick and Painless Loan Approval

If you require a new mortgage to finance your purchase, the sales contract probably contains your promise to apply promptly at a lending institution. The real estate broker can often suggest the lender most favorable to your situation and the seller's. It might be the one that asks the fewest points this week, processes applications promptly or looks with favor on unusual older houses. Or you may be relying on a mortgage broker.

In some areas, the agent makes the appointment for you and accompanies you to the application session. If you are on your own, sit down with the yellow pages open to "Mortgages" and ask to speak with a mortgage counselor or mortgage loan officer. Do your own research.

Come to the application session armed with as many facts as possible. The lender will want to know a great deal about your financial situation, all aimed at not letting you get in over your head in debt.

Factors the underwriters will consider in deciding whether or not to make the loan are: employment stability and other dependable income, your present assets, credit history, past mortgage payment experience and present debts.

The lender judges two things: your ability to meet your obligations in the future and your willingness to do so, as evidenced in the past.

What To Take to the Interview

To expedite your application, take as much as possible to your initial interview.

You will need an original purchase contract signed by all parties; it will be copied and returned to you. Bring the seller's agreement to pay points (if not in the contract).

Plan to bring cash or check for your application fee, to cover appraisal of the property and credit report. Additional points or origination fee may be required.

Have your Social Security number and a list of all your income, assets, debts and credit cards, with account numbers and balances. Take the addresses of out-of-town creditors. The interviewer will ask for account numbers and balances on checking and saving accounts, with branch addresses.

Provide information on two years' past employment and two years' past addresses. If self-employed, you'll need two years' signed income-tax returns, if you've been on your job less than two years, copies of previous W-2s.

If you are a landlord, bring expense and income statements on property presently rented out, and leases signed by tenants.

Also necessary: donor's name and address for gift letter; explanation of any credit problems; copies of bankruptcy papers; Certificate of Eligibility, if applying for VA loan; legal description of property, survey (not required for all loans); true property tax figure on the projected purchase; name and phone number of person who will give access to the lending institution's appraiser; copy of divorce decree or separation agreement if paying child support or alimony; same documents if claiming them for income, along with proof that payments are being received. The more documents you bring to your mortgage application appointment, the more smoothly the process will run.

Assets Required

You must show you have enough cash on hand for the estimated closing costs on your loan and often for a payment or two after that. Beyond that, your list of assets, particularly in a border-line situation, will influence the underwriters when they're deciding if it's safe to make the loan.

You may not borrow elsewhere for the down payment (secondary financing) on most loans. Lenders are skeptical about claims that your money is under the mattress and will credit you with only a limited amount in cash—as little as $200, perhaps. They will also want an explanation for large sums of money that have suddenly turned up in your savings accounts within the past few months. (Maybe, they figure, you borrowed it somewhere, thus taking on too much debt.)

Bring in all details on your assets: numbers and balances on savings accounts (the lender will check with the bank to verify), list of stocks and bonds owned, income tax return if you anticipate a refund. Your earnest money deposit counts as an asset; the lender will verify it with the person holding it.

You may have assets you've forgotten about: cash surrender value on your life insurance policy, valuable collections, jewelry, boats and RVs, IRA accounts, other real estate owned. List your furniture, appliances and automobiles; they might not bring much if you sold them, but they prove that you won't need to go on a buying spree right after you close on the house.

A gift letter from a relative, promising to furnish some of the funds you need for closing with no repayment required or anticipated, can sometimes be used at mortgage application. Many lenders require the letter on their own form, and most want to verify that the relative does indeed have the funds in question.

Income That Counts

Just about any kind of income can be used to qualify, if it can be counted on in the future and can be verified. More than one borrower (husband and wife or unrelated buyers) may pool their incomes to qualify for the loan.

Ideally, two years' continuous employment in the same field indicates employment stability. Exceptions are made for recent graduates or those who have just left the armed forces. Lenders are nervous about those who jump often from one sort of job to another; employment changes that show upward movement within the same field are more acceptable.

Bonuses and overtime count toward qualification if your employer will verify them as dependable. Part-time and commission income count if they have been steady for the past year or two. Alimony and child support can be considered as income if you want to claim them, but you must be able to show that they are being paid dependably and are likely to continue for the next five years or so.

Older applicants will not be asked their ages but will be asked to prove dependable Social Security and pension income if they anticipate retirement within the next few years. Disability income is counted if it is permanent.

Those on seasonal income may count it if they can prove at least a two-year history of such a cycle, and they may even be able to count unemployment insurance in qualifying.

The self-employed will be asked to furnish income-tax returns for two years past and, where it's appropriate, an audited profit-and-loss statement.

Other sources of income might include dividends and interest, and net rental from other properties (leases signed by your tenants may be required). If you will have rental income from the house you are buying (a duplex, for example, with the other side to be rented out) half or even all of the anticipated rent may be counted as further income.

With special programs specifically intended to help good applicants who might not otherwise qualify, some programs allow lenders to be more flexible—not requiring two years' record of some income, for example, or taking into consideration the rent you've been managing to pay.

Analyzing Your Debts

Lenders give careful consideration to your present debts, your liabilities. Depending on the type of loan for which you are applying, they will count any debt on which you must pay for more than 6, 10 or 12 months. Car loans are among the most common liabilities in this category.

Before you arrive for mortgage application, list your liabilities, including loan numbers, monthly payment, balances and time left to run. Student loans are considered obligations if payments are presently due. Child support or alimony is considered an obligation; so is child care, for VA or FHA loans.

Watch out for credit cards. Some lenders, for some mortgage plans, may consider that you are liable for the potential full borrowing power on each of them. That can be true even if you don't carry balances (see page 42).

Your assets, debts and income allow the lender to judge whether you can make the proposed mortgage payments. Their final question is: Are you not only able but willing to meet your obligations? That's where your credit history comes in.

It is essential to divulge information about past credit problems frankly during your interview. You should already have discussed judgments or bankruptcies with the real estate agent during your first meeting. Such problems won't necessarily prevent you from obtaining a mortgage, but if the lender's checking turns up any lies, you're in trouble.

To find out about your credit history, simply go to your local credit bureau and draw an inexpensive or free report on yourself (see Chapter 1). Do it early on. If any inaccuracies show up, the bureau will help you clear them up.

If you've never borrowed money before, don't worry. An old wives' tale says you must take out a loan and repay it to establish credit. Lenders know, though, that you've been around long enough to get into trouble if you were going to. No credit history is considered good credit history.

Less-than-perfect credit may qualify you for one sort of loan and not another. VA and FHA guidelines are generally more lenient, though banks making their own portfolio loans can be flexible within certain limits. In the mid '90s, the federal government sparked many community mortgage plans aimed at helping less-than-perfect first-time buyers qualify.

The lender may ask you for written explanations of slow payment history or any derogatory report. You will have to pay off any open judgments, even if they flow from an "I won't pay as a matter of principle" dispute.

Bankruptcy guidelines vary, depending on the type of bankruptcy and type of loan. In general, one to two years must have elapsed since the discharge of your bankruptcy, though each case is considered separately. If your problem was due to something beyond your control and your previous credit history was exemplary, exceptions can be made. Most important is your record of payments on any previous mortgage loan.

You'll be asked to sign a number of papers when you apply for the loan, many of them authorizing the release of verifying information from your employer, savings institution or credit bureau. You'll also be asked for an application fee, which covers a credit report on yourself and an appraisal of the property. Sometimes other up-front fees are requested. In a time of rising interest rates, for example, you could be offered a chance to lock in the current rate for the payment of one point.

After the Application

As you approach the next phase of your adventure, watch out for a malady known by the scientific name of Buyer's Remorse. Onset may be from 24 hours to two weeks after your purchase offer was accepted. Symptoms usually develop rapidly around 2 AM, as you lie awake wondering why you ever got into this, if you can really afford the house, how you will get along without your present neighbors and whether the whole thing isn't a big mistake.

Buyer's Remorse is akin to the last-minute jitters that afflict brides and grooms before the wedding. One consolation: If it's all a big mistake, selling a house will be simpler than getting a divorce.

Rather than lose any more sleep, call the real estate broker the next day asking to visit the house again, preferably when the sellers are absent. In nearly every case, the buyer is pleasantly surprised during the return visit. All that hard work, the research, the exhausting house-hunting, really did pay off; this is clearly the best house in town for you. If, as happens rarely, you are more depressed than ever after your return visit, it's time for a conference with your attorney to determine your legal position if you back out and how much money you stand to forfeit.

Monitoring the Application

While the lending institution completes all the paperwork ("assembling the exhibits"), the real estate agent should keep in touch in case any hitches develop. You might check yourself from time to time to see if things are going smoothly. Lenders have even been known to lose a whole file, so that everything has to be done over again!

Within three days of your application, the lending institution must send you a good faith estimate of your closing costs and notification of your APR, the annual percentage rate. If you paid for the appraisal, you are entitled to receive a copy; if it isn't offered, request it in writing.

Keep the broker, or your lawyer, informed of any communication you receive from the lending institution, local government or FHA. Above all, don't go out and buy a car. This is not the time to incur additional debt or deplete your cash.

If you have questions for the seller, it's usually best to ask them through the broker, who can arrange for you to measure for curtains or show the place to your parents. Experience has proven that the transaction proceeds most efficiently when the broker and lawyers handle communication between buyer and seller. There are exceptions, of course; sellers have been known to host a barbecue to introduce the buyers to the neighbors.

After all the exhibits have been assembled, the lender's mortgage committee reviews the underwriting decision. It may then issue either a full commitment or a conditional commitment letter dependent, for example, on certain repairs being made to the property before closing or on your clearing up an outstanding judgment. In any event, be sure to contact the broker and your lawyer or closing agent as soon as you hear from the lender.

Once you have the commitment safely in hand, nothing remains but to find a time (within the number of days stipulated in the commitment letter) that suits everyone for transferring the property. You are ready for closing.

Moving in Before Closing

You'll find sellers—and particularly sellers' attorneys—very reluctant to let you move in before you actually own the home. If you absolutely must take possession in an emergency situation, be prepared for some complicated paperwork.

In the same fashion, by the way, sellers and their attorneys may be unwilling to let you do any painting or make any improvements, even if the house is vacant. There's always a danger that something might go wrong and they'd be left still owning the house with half-finished renovations on their hands.

If, on the other hand, you had been over there at night putting in new kitchen cabinets and your purchase fell apart at the last minute, you'd have lost your labor and materials. Anything you do to improve someone else's property becomes part of the real estate and you'd have no claim for the money you spent.

How the Agent Can Help

Most real estate agents can give you up-to-date information on the local availability of various mortgage plans, sometimes by computer search. Many agents will set up an application interview with the lender you choose and, again, this can sometimes be done by computer contact.

While you're waiting for a mortgage commitment, both sellers' and buyers' agents expect to keep a close eye on the process, and to handle problems that may turn up. The agent may also arrange your return visit to the property. If the property "fails to appraise" and the lender offers only a lesser amount than you need, the agent may arrange for a re-appraisal, furnish comps to back up your purchase price, or even suggest applying at a different institution. In some cases, you'll be asked to re-negotiate your contract.

☞ **Money-Saving Tip #39** *If the bank's appraisal comes in for a lower figure than your purchase price, the seller may agree to renegotiate.*

Commonly Asked Questions

Q. Do student loans count as debts against me?

A. Only if you're already paying on them or if you are in default on them..

Q. Why does it matter how many credit cards I have?

A. Because you could conceivably borrow to the limit on all of them, thus taking on an unacceptable amount of debt.

Q. What if I work "off the books" and my income tax returns don't reflect my true income?

A. Lenders won't count any income you can't verify.

CHAPTER 11

Preparing for a Hassle-Free Closing Day

In few real estate matters does local custom vary so widely as in final transfer of title, the day when you actually pay for the property and become the owner.

Closings may be conducted by attorneys, title companies, escrow services, lending institutions, even in some areas by real estate brokers. They may take place at the county courthouse, a bank, title company, attorney's office or other location. Sometimes everyone sits around a big table; sometimes buyer and seller never even meet. The process could be called going to escrow, running a closing or (in some parts of New England) passing papers.

The Closing Process

If you're placing a new mortgage, you'll be asked to prepay interest for the rest of the present month, to bring you up to the lender's usual "first of the month" bookkeeping. That means that if you close early in the month, you'll need that much more cash. It isn't really an extra cost, of course, because you'll own the property from that day on. Still, between that and the rent you're paying, you might prefer to close toward the end of the month.

You won't, by the way, need to make any mortgage payment on the first of the next month, because mortgage interest is normally paid in arrears (the opposite of in advance.) Close in June, prepay interest up to June 30, and you won't owe any July payment, because that would have been for use of the money during the month of June, and you paid that at closing. Your first payment will be due in August and will cover July's interest.

Title Insurance Policies

Your purchase contract provides a blueprint for the final transfer. The seller's main responsibility is to prove title, to show that you are receiving clear and trouble-free ownership. Depending on the mortgagee's requirements and local custom, the seller may prove title by furnishing an abstract and lawyer's opinion, title insurance or, in some cities and states, Torrens certificate.

☞ **Money-$aving Tip #40** *If the present owner has a title insurance policy less than three years old, you could have substantial savings by buying a reissue of that policy rather than a completely new one.*

Two types of title insurance are available. One, which may be required by your lender, protects the mortgagee—the lender—against loss if other parties challenge your ownership. If you need the policy for your mortgage loan, you may be asked to pay for it. The premium is a single payment, good for the whole time you own the property. For a relatively small additional fee, you can purchase at the same time an owner's policy, which protects you from loss if anyone challenges your ownership.

An abstract is a history of all transactions affecting the property that is researched from the public records. Typically, the seller must furnish an up-to-date abstract and forward it to you (better yet, to your attorney) for inspection before the closing to make sure no problems exist. Where closings are handled by escrow or title companies, many of the same procedures are followed within the company.

The third method of proving title, the Torrens system, is used in some cities and states and provides a central, permanent registration of title to the property.

Unrelated Persons Buying Together

If two or more persons are buying together, the wording of the deed determines their respective shares of ownership, their legal rights and the disposition of the property upon the death of one of them. Depending on state law, three types of joint ownership are possible.

1. Under *tenancy in common,* each owner has the right to leave his or her share to his estate or to chosen heirs.
2. With *joint tenancy with right of survivorship,* if one owner dies, the surviving owner(s) automatically take over that share.
3. *Tenancy by the entirety* is a special form of joint tenancy for married couples.

If the owners are to have unequal shares, tenancy in common is the usual form. Except with tenancy by the entirety, any owner has the right to force a division or sale of the property (partition) in the future.

When there is more than one owner, it is important to check with an attorney to make sure the deed clearly states the desired form of ownership. If you are unmarried cobuyers, be sure to decide in advance what you'd want to happen if one of you died. Do you want the other to become complete owner, or do you each want the right to leave your share to someone else?

Purpose of the Deed

A deed, when signed by the owner of real estate, states that the property is being transferred to a new owner. The deed, the bill of sale for real estate, is drawn up ahead of time so that it can be examined and approved. A full *warranty* deed contains legal guarantees: that the seller really owns the property, for example, and that no one will ever challenge your right to it. In some areas, the standard is a *bargain and sale deed* with covenant, or *special warranty* deed, that contains some guarantees but not as many. If you buy from an estate, you receive an *executor's* deed. A *quit-claim* deed completely transfers whatever ownership the grantor (person signing the deed) may have had, but it makes no binding guarantees of ownership in the first place.

You become owner at the exact moment when the deed is handed to you and accepted by you—physical transfer of a document that represents the real estate you are buying.

As You Get Ready for Closing

You'll be alerted a few days before closing as to the exact amount of money needed. Cash or a certified check is usually required; no one wants to turn over so valuable an asset on a personal check. Except where you won't be in attendance (escrow closing), it's simplest to have a certified check or money order made out to your attorney or yourself. You can always endorse it, and matters are simpler if anything goes wrong. Bring a supply of your personal checks as well for small matters that may come up at the last minute.

You will probably be asked to bring proof that you are placing insurance on the property. Real estate in a flood-prone area may be required to carry flood insurance. If you have difficulty finding a local lender for flood insurance, contact the National Flood Insurance Program at 1-800-638-6620.

As closing approaches, request a last-minute walk-through of the property. If you see a window that was broken since you first inspected the house or a junked car in the backyard, don't talk directly with the seller. Instead, contact the agent and your lawyer immediately.

At closing, you are handed one paper after another, accompanied by a brief whispered explanation that you're too excited to understand and the words "sign here." In some areas, on the other hand, buyer and seller sign all the documents ahead of time, and when everything is in order, an escrow agent, who holds all the papers, declares the transfer has taken place.

If you are assuming a mortgage, you will receive a reduction certificate, the lender's statement that the principal has been paid down to a certain amount. You should receive proof that the payments are current and that property taxes are paid up to date. A last-minute title search will reassure you that the seller did not borrow money against the property earlier that morning.

Watch Out for Problems

It's extremely important to have last-minute problems cleared up before you hand over your check or the lenders'. Once transfer of title has taken place, many matters are *merged* into the closing—you have bought the problems along with the property. Don't rely, then, on promises that something will be taken care of "in the next few days." If it is impractical to solve the problem immediately, ask that part of the purchase price be held in escrow to be turned over to the seller only after the matter is attended to.

When Do You Move In?

In most parts of the country, it is assumed that possession will be given you on the day of closing; in a few areas it's customary to allow the seller a few days after closing to move out.

If you agree to let the sellers remain in occupancy after closing, be sure they have plenty of financial motivation to move out as promised. Otherwise, you could find yourself stuck with a lengthy and expensive eviction. Per diem rental should be set at a high figure, with the provision that it will be deducted from that part of the purchase price held in escrow pending the seller's vacating as agreed. Sometimes the rent figure is set up to increase if they don't leave when they're supposed to.

Prorations and Adjustments

Many small items must be apportioned fairly between you and the seller. Your state will assume that the owner on the day of closing is either seller or buyer. Items adjusted as of the date of closing might include property taxes, interest in a mortgage being assumed or unpaid water bills.

If the tenants in the attic apartment have paid rent for the present month, part of that rent may belong to you. You should receive the security deposit they paid, because some day they will ask you to return it.

When all items are listed on a balance sheet, you'll receive full credit for the earnest money deposit you placed with the real estate agent. If the lender requires a trust account, you'll be asked to place in escrow several months' property taxes and insurance costs, mortgage insurance or other items.

Various sums charged to either buyer or seller may include recording fees (for the new deed and mortgage), attorney's fees, transfer tax (revenue stamps), notary fees, charges for document preparation, mortgage tax and closing agent's fee.

The Real Estate Settlement Procedures Act (RESPA) requires a uniform statement to be furnished to you. See the sample RESPA statement on page 142. In addition, your attorney or the person handling the closing should furnish you with a simpler account of your expenses and credits.

Documents You'll Sign

You'll find yourself signing two papers for the mortgage. One is the bond, or note, the personal promise to repay the loan. The other is the mortgage (or deed of trust) itself, the financial lien (claim) against the property, that gives the lender the right to foreclose if you default. Then the mortgagee gives you a check, probably the largest you'll ever see. You get to hold it just long enough to endorse it and turn it over to the seller.

The deed, which is signed only by the grantor (the seller), will be placed in your hands and then taken away to be recorded. It will probably be sent to you later. If no one is available to record the deed, take it to the county recorder (usually the county clerk) and record it yourself immediately; this is of utmost importance.

You will also receive all the keys, the garage door opener and the code for the security system. Many buyers like to have their locks changed as soon as they move in. You would do the same, of course, with the code on any security system.

RESPA UNIFORM SETTLEMENT STATEMENT

A. Settlement Statement

U.S. Department of Housing
and Urban Development

OMB Approval No. 2502-0265

B. Type of Loan

1. ☐ FHA 2. ☐ FmHA 3. ☐ Conv. Unins.
4. ☐ VA 5. ☐ Conv. Ins.

6. File Number	7. Loan Number	8. Mortgage Insurance Case Number

C. Note: This form is furnished to give you a statement of actual settlement costs. Amounts paid to and by the settlement agent are shown. Items marked "(p.o.c.)" were paid outside the closing; they are shown here for informational purposes and are not included in the totals.

D. Name and Address of Borrower	E. Name and Address of Seller	F. Name and Address of Lender

G. Property Location	H. Settlement Agent	
	Place of Settlement	I. Settlement Date

J. Summary of Borrower's Transaction		K. Summary of Seller's Transaction	
100. Gross Amount Due From Borrower		**400. Gross Amount Due To Seller**	
101. Contract sales price		401. Contract sales price	
102. Personal property		402. Personal property	
103. Settlement charges to borrower (line 1400)		403.	
104.		404.	
105.		405.	
Adjustments for items paid by seller in advance		*Adjustments for items paid by seller in advance*	
106. City/town taxes to		406. City/town taxes to	
107. County taxes to		407. County taxes to	
108. Assessments to		408. Assessments to	
109.		409.	
110.		410.	
111.		411.	
112.		412.	
120. Gross Amount Due From Borrower		**420. Gross Amount Due To Seller**	
200. Amounts Paid By Or In Behalf Of Borrower		**500. Reductions In Amount Due To Seller**	
201. Deposit or earnest money		501. Excess deposit (see instructions)	
202. Principal amount of new loan(s)		502. Settlement charges to seller (line 1400)	
203. Existing loan(s) taken subject to		503. Existing loan(s) taken subject to	
204.		504. Payoff of first mortgage loan	
205.		505. Payoff of second mortgage loan	
206.		506.	
207.		507.	
208.		508.	
209.		509.	
Adjustments for items unpaid by seller		*Adjustments for items unpaid by seller*	
210. City/town taxes to		510. City/town taxes to	
211. County taxes to		511. County taxes to	
212. Assessments to		512. Assessments to	
213.		513.	
214.		514.	
215.		515.	
216.		516.	
217.		517.	
218.		518.	
219.		519.	
220. Total Paid By/For Borrower		**520. Total Reduction Amount Due Seller**	
300. Cash At Settlement From/To Borrower		**600. Cash At Settlement To/From Seller**	
301. Gross Amount due from borrower (line 120)		601. Gross amount due to seller (line 420)	
302. Less amounts paid by/for borrower (line 220)	( )	602. Less reductions in amt. due seller (line 520)	( )
303. Cash ☐ From ☐ To Borrower		**603. Cash** ☐ To ☐ From Seller	

L. Settlement Charges

		Paid From Borrowers Funds at Settlement	Paid From Seller's Funds at Settlement
700. Total Sales/Broker's Commission based on price $ @ % =			
Division of Commission (line 700) as follows:			
701. $ to			
702. $ to			
703. Commission paid at Settlement			
704.			
800. Items Payable In Connection With Loan			
801. Loan Origination Fee %			
802. Loan Discount %			
803. Appraisal Fee to			
804. Credit Report to			
805. Lender's Inspection Fee			
806. Mortgage Insurance Application Fee to			
807. Assumption Fee			
808.			
809.			
810.			
811.			
900. Items Required By Lender To Be Paid In Advance			
901. Interest from to @$ /day			
902. Mortgage Insurance Premium for months to			
903. Hazard Insurance Premium for years to			
904. years to			
905.			
1000. Reserves Deposited With Lender			
1001. Hazard insurance months@$ per month			
1002. Mortgage insurance months@$ per month			
1003. City property taxes months@$ per month			
1004. County property taxes months@$ per month			
1005. Annual assessments months@$ per month			
1006. months@$ per month			
1007. months@$ per month			
1008. months@$ per month			
1100. Title Charges			
1101. Settlement or closing fee to			
1102. Abstract or title search to			
1103. Title examination to			
1104. Title insurance binder to			
1105. Document preparation to			
1106. Notary fees to			
1107. Attorney's fees to			
(includes above items numbers:)			
1108. Title insurance to			
(includes above items numbers:)			
1109. Lender's coverage $			
1110. Owner's coverage $			
1111.			
1112.			
1113.			
1200. Government Recording and Transfer Charges			
1201. Recording fees: Deed $; Mortgage $; Releases $			
1202. City/county tax/stamps: Deed $; Mortgage $			
1203. State tax/stamps: Deed $; Mortgage $			
1204.			
1205.			
1300. Additional Settlement Charges			
1301. Survey to			
1302. Pest inspection to			
1303.			
1304.			
1305.			
1400. Total Settlement Charges (enter on lines 103, Section J and 502, Section K)			

Public Reporting Burden for this collection of information is estimated to average 0.25 hours per response, including the time for reviewing instructions, searching existing data sources, gathering and maintaining the data needed, and completing and reviewing the collection of information. Send comments regarding this burden estimate or any other aspect of this collection of information, including suggestions for reducing this burden, to the Reports Management Officer, Office of Information Policies and Systems, U.S. Department of Housing and Urban Development, Washington, D.C. 20410-3600, and to the Office of Management and Budget, Paperwork Reduction Project (2502-0265), Washington, D.C. 20503

U.S. GOVERNMENT PRINTING OFFICE 1989 0-944-245

How the Agent Can Help

An agent's job is far from over when you have signed a purchase contract and applied for a loan. Until you have a firm mortgage commitment, the agent will keep in touch with the lending institution, arrange any necessary inspections and check about any missing paperwork.

If you receive a conditional commitment, stating that the loan will be made only if certain repairs are completed on the property, the agent will monitor the process and arrange for a reinspection when the work is done satisfactorily.

As the closing approaches, the agent will help you estimate the cash you need to take to the settlement session for closing costs. The agent will arrange your last-minute walk-through and help solve any problems that surface at that point. In some parts of the country, it is customary for any agents involved to attend the closing.

Commonly Asked Questions

Q. Does it matter what day we close?

A. Because you will pay interest, taxes and insurance from the day you close, you'd probably prefer a closing that dovetails with your present lease, so that you won't end up paying expenses on two different places for part or all of a month. On the other hand, you may want a few days with the new house vacant, for repainting or other projects.

Although it may affect the amount of actual cash you need, the day of the month you choose won't make any difference in your costs.

Q. Why doesn't a deed mention the house I'm buying?

A. You are buying real estate, and any building on the parcel described in the deed goes with the land. Deeds almost never make any mention of buildings.

Q. I have a deed to the lot I bought but no deed to the house I built on it. How do I solve this?

A. See the previous question. There's no one to give you a deed to the house, and you don't need one.

Q. What happens if I lose my deed?

A. Once you have received the deed and had it entered in the public records, it has no further function. If you ever wanted a copy, you could obtain it from your county recorder.

CHAPTER 12

Moving into Your New Home

$\mathbf{A}$s the old saying goes, "A move is as good as a fire"—for shaking up your life and clearing out your belongings.

Change-of-Address Cards

Early on, make a list of people to be notified about your change of address. Besides friends and relatives, send change-of-address cards (available at the post office) to professionals like your physician, dentist, accountant, attorney and stock-broker; ask for transfers of records if you are leaving town. Request records also if you or your children are changing schools.

Send change-of-address notices to magazines several weeks in advance. Notify your bank; you may want to close out accounts. Give your new address to your charge card companies, insurance companies, your church and your union. Notify the motor vehicle bureau, post office, Department of Veterans Affairs, Social Security administration, income tax bureau and voter registration.

Notify the post office of your moving date, and if necessary ask that your mail be held until you send written instructions to forward it. First-class mail will be forwarded free for one year; publications and parcel post items are forwarded only if you agree to pay any extra postage due.

Services To Cut Off

As soon as you know your moving date, notify the telephone company, water service, gas and electric company, and arrange for final readings of meters. Remember to cut off anything that is delivered to your home: fuel oil, newspapers, diaper service. Notify service persons who call regularly for pest control, trash collection, landscaping, water softener service or pool maintenance.

Investigate refunds that may be due on your present prepaid renters or homeowners insurance, prepaid cable service, and deposits for utilities or deposits with your landlord. Tie up loose ends: Return library books, empty lockers, pick up dry cleaning.

Look over Your Belongings

Take a good look at the contents of your present home. When a moving company has given you a rough estimate of its charge per 100 pounds, you can decide for yourself whether you should plan on moving that five-pound bag of sugar and the old refrigerator or just buy replacements at your new location.

☞ **Money-$aving Tip #41** *Consider how much it costs per pound to move items and calculate how much cheaper it might be merely to replace them later.*

A garage sale is of course the first step. Be prepared: Antique dealers and determined garage sale addicts will arrive at least an hour before your advertisement states. To questions about whether you'll take less than the price you've posted for an item, you might respond that you'll offer whatever is left at half price on the afternoon of your final sale day. Items that don't sell can be donated to charity; ask for a receipt if the donation qualifies for a tax deduction.

If You Are Moving Yourself

As a self-mover, you could end up with more breakage than trained professional movers might incur and, of course, could put yourself at risk for injury or liability for your helpful friends' accidents. And there's always the possibility of an accident with a truck you're not used to driving. But you do save money.

Rental agencies can furnish material to help estimate what size truck or trailer you will need. They can also rent you a hand truck or dolly, furniture pads and straps. Expect to pay a daily charge for a trailer and a daily charge plus mileage for a truck. Your rental can be round-trip or one-way, with a drop-off at the nearest point to your destination. If your move is out of town, consider gasoline costs as well as tolls. Some road taxes may be involved.

Most rental companies will accept credit cards; professional moving companies seldom do. You will be asked to make a refundable deposit for the material you rent.

Insurance on the Move

Whether you are moving on your own or hiring a professional company, be sure to check on insurance coverage for lost or damaged items and injuries to yourself or others.

Find out what insurance the movers or rental agencies carry, and consult your own agent to see whether your present policy covers the move, whether you have a floater for valuable items, whether you would receive replacement or full value for losses. Consider buying additional temporary insurance to increase whatever you, the moving company or the rental company carry, if necessary.

Using a Professional Moving Company

If you plan to use a professional moving service, it's wise to make a videotape record of your possessions before the move. It's also prudent to call three reputable moving companies to ask for estimates, and it won't hurt to let them know you're also talking with their competitors. While standard tariff rates are published, discounts are possible. Expect to pay extra for deliveries on evenings, weekends or holidays, unless it's the driver who requests them.

Movers charge extra for certain large items like pianos. You'll pay extra for packing and unpacking, disassembly or assembly and for any additional storage days you request before unloading. The estimator will also take into consideration any staircases involved.

Some shipments are transferred to another company for a long-distance move. Try to find a company that will make a direct shipment, which is less expensive and easier on your furniture.

Order for Service

Your order for service (which is not a contract and can be cancelled) is filled out when you decide to use a particular company. It should include a complete description of all the items involved, though you can later add or delete with an addendum. (Your driver might later refuse to take any item not on the list.)

The contract, which states everyone's responsibilities, is the bill of lading you will later be asked to sign. Look it over first to make sure it matches the estimate and service order.

The Move Itself

Movers determine the weight of your shipment by weighing the truck before and after it is loaded. If delivery isn't made when promised, you may be reimbursed for any extra expenses you incurred.

Movers require payment in cash or certified check before they will unload. If your bill is more than 10 percent over the estimate, you need pay only the original fee to take delivery; the rest is usually due within 30 days.

It's best to monitor the unloading, checking the inventory yourself and noting any disagreements you may have about the condition of the items. Don't sign off on the delivery until you are satisfied that the paperwork is accurate. A second "after" videotape is excellent for inventory and reference purposes and, along with photographs, is useful for documenting damages. You might need to file a claim after the move for missing items and damages and for extra expenses that were not your fault.

Do Your Own Packing

If you are using professional movers, you can save by doing a great deal of the packing on your own. Rental companies and movers themselves sell cartons of uniform sizes that stack easily, suitable for clothing, china and other specific uses. Sturdy cartons are available from liquor stores, heavy larger ones from computer stores.

You may prefer to pack only unbreakable items, leaving the china and lamps to the professionals.

For heavy items that you won't need right away, you might investigate slower freight companies, at lower cost. Be sure to use smaller boxes for books and other heavy items. Label each box with an indelible marker, indicating which room the box should be unloaded into.

Fill dresser drawers with pillows. Empty water from your refrigerator pan and steam iron. Pack suitcases for each family member, with clothing for the first few days. Pack one box to be loaded last or taken in your car, with items you'll need when you move in. Include cleaning supplies and rags, extension cords, hammer and screwdriver, paper plates and cups and plastic silverware, saucepan, coffee maker and supplies, children's toys, snacks, toothbrushes, toothpaste, soap and towels.

Your important documents can go in a portable file case and travel with you, along with your jewelry. If your car is making the move, that may be the right place for whatever plants you haven't given away.

Be sure to leave your new address and, if you know it, your new telephone number conspicuously posted so the next occupants of your home can forward mail and phone calls. When you arrange utility service at your new home, inquire about installation of appliances.

Income Tax and Moving Expenses

If your move is closely related to a new job or a job transfer, you may be eligible to deduct some moving expenses provided that your new job is at least 50 miles further from your old home than your old job was; or if you had no previous job, your new one is at least 50 miles from your old home; or if you are in the armed forces and had a permanent change of station. To qualify, you must work full-time in the new location. If you are self-employed, you may still qualify to deduct moving expenses if you work at least 39 weeks in each of the next two years in the new location.

Deductible Moving Expenses

If you meet the requirements outlined above, you can deduct everything you spend for

- packing, crating and transporting household goods and personal effects for your whole household;
- nine cents a mile for use of your own car in moving goods, yourself or members of your household (or, if you choose, actual gas and oil expenses you keep track of);
- tolls and parking fees paid during the trip;
- storing and insuring household goods and personal effects for 30 days during the move;
- disconnecting and connecting utilities;
- cost of shipping your car or pets;
- transportation and lodging for yourself and members of your household while traveling to the new home. Cost for meals is not included.

The expenses listed above are all fully deductible, but can cover only a *single one-way trip*—the actual move itself.

How *the Agent Can Help*

If you are relocating, agents can help on both ends, particularly in the new location where you may not yet have friends to assist. An agent can give you help in signing up for utilities, phone and cable at the new home, and can arrange to have the door unlocked for appraisers or inspectors. The agent can also put you in touch with cleaning services or other help you may want before you arrive.

Commonly Asked Questions

Q. Can I deduct my moving costs on my income tax return even if I take a standard deduction?

A. Yes, if you qualify as described in this chapter.

Q. What sort of expenses are usually covered when the new employer offers reimbursement for my move?

A. That varies. It helps to have the agreement in writing. Ask whether there's a maxiumum reimbursement and whether it covers interviews, house-hunting trips, hotel or motel if needed in the new location.

Q. Where can I get brochures on moving?

A. You can call local franchised movers or United Van Lines at 1-800-325-3870.

CHAPTER 13

Decreasing Your Tax Bite

No other investment gives you the marvelous tax shelters you get with your home. You can deduct points paid for your loan in the first year, you get to deduct almost all the carrying costs of the home (interest and taxes) while you are living in it, and when you sell it's easy to postpone your taxable profit, and in some cases, never pay tax on it at all. When it comes to tax benefits, no other investment even comes close.

The information in this chapter applies to federal income tax only. Tax law about deductible items may vary from one state to another. It is wise, in the year you buy or sell your home, to have professional assistance with your tax return. Individual situations differ, and all of the information in this chapter should be checked with your own accountant, CPA or enrolled agent. It is possible, for example, that your deductions in general will be limited once your adjusted gross income exceeds a certain amount.

When in Doubt, Don't Throw It Out

To make the most of federal income tax provisions, you need to know your way around the maze of regulations. But how can you tell exactly what figures to enter (or give to your accountant)? Equally important, how can you prove what you have claimed, if your return is ever audited? Your first step is to keep proper records and keep proper documentation. And you should start before another day has passed.

What To Save

From an Internal Revenue Service (IRS) point of view, a cancelled check for $200 to your electrician may not prove anything. Who knows? It could represent his winnings in your last poker game. For tax purposes, you need not only prove that the money was spent, but also prove that it was spent for the purpose you claim. So save your invoices and receipted bills.

If your bank no longer returns cancelled checks, it's particularly important to be careful about keeping check stubs. You can also mark up your monthly statement while your memory is fresh. If you ever need to substantiate your tax return, your bank can furnish copies of the specific check numbers you request. Do the same thing with tax-relevant items on your monthly credit card statement.

Save your income tax returns also. They serve as a time-saving guide for the next year's return, and you may need to refer to them in years to come. When you buy your home, stash every scrap of paper you receive in a folder labelled "Closing."

How Long To Keep Records

You have up to three years in which to amend an income tax return, starting from the date the tax is due, April 15.

The IRS also uses the three-year limit for its routine audits. Where it suspects underreported income of at least 25 percent, it can extend inquiries back six years. And if fraud is in question, it can go back forever.

Most accountants recommend seven years as a minimum for retaining documents, checks, stubs and statements, to cover the three-year and six-year periods. Where your home is concerned, the minimum should be "at least seven years after you sell the house."

Beyond that, if you roll over profit for postponed tax when you sell, keep everything related to the cost of that first house and its sale, until at least seven years after you sell the *next* home. And if you roll over again, keep the documents for each and every house in the chain. Accountants say they feel most secure when you keep papers "forever."

Definition of Home

The IRS uses the word in its broadest sense. Your home may be a condominium, mobile home, houseboat, cooperative apartment, castle or log cabin, if it has sleeping and cooking facilities. Your main home is the place where you live most of the time.

It may be only part of a house, with the rest classified as business property or a rental unit. In that case, homeowner's tax treatments will apply to only a percentage of the building, whether for yearly tax returns or at the time of sale. The rest of the building will be classified as business or rental property, with separate tax reporting.

Vacant land doesn't qualify for homeowner's tax breaks, even if it's a lot on which you intend to build or a wilderness retreat on which you pitch a tent. Property taxes are completely deductible, but beyond that no special interest deduction or capital gains treatment applies for vacant land.

The IRS defines your main home, or principal residence, as the one you occupy most of the time. Except in rare and unusual cases, that is the only test they apply.

Home Ownership Tax Breaks

Some tax breaks are available every year on your tax return. In general, property taxes and mortgage insurance are deductible yearly, with some limitations that don't affect most persons. Other possibilities for yearly deductions include job hunting and moving expenses, mortgage points, interest on special property tax assessments and casualty losses.

Tax Breaks at Sale

Tax shelter for profit on the sale of one's main home generally takes one of two forms: rollover or one-time exclusion.

Rollover. A taxpayer of any age is allowed to postpone tax on all or part of profit when one main home is sold and replaced within two years by another. Capital gains tax is not forgiven forever; it is simply postponed until the next home is sold. At that point it is often postponed again in the same manner, piling up untaxed profit on a string of homes.

One-time exclusion. Senior citizens have a one-time opportunity to sell and take up to $125,000 profit free of any federal income tax ever. Briefly, the owner must

- be 55 or older on the date of sale,
- have owned and occupied the house as a principal residence for at least three of the five years before the sale,
- have never used this one-time exclusion before, and

* not be married, on the date of sale, to anyone who ever used it previously.

You decide when you want to use this once-in-a-lifetime exclusion. It applies whether or not you buy a replacement residence. The $125,000 limit can include untaxed piled-up profit on a string of previous homes for which you rolled over your capital gain. (If your profit is very high, you can even combine the two tax treatments, using the exclusion on the first $125,000 of your profit and rolling over the rest for postponement.)

☞ **Money-$aving Tip #42** *If you qualify, the $125,000 exclusion is available whether or not you buy a replacement residence, for substantial tax savings.*

Papers on the Closing Table

From an income tax point of view, your closing papers are important for two reasons. They establish your initial *cost basis* for the property, and they may help reduce taxable profit when you eventually sell.

They may also be needed if some day you change some or all of your home to a home office, business or rental property.

For This Year's Taxes

Some of the money you lay out when you buy can be used as an immediate deduction on this year's income tax return. Among the most important are "points," representing extra up-front interest on a mortgage loan to buy your own home, and property taxes.

Cost Basis Starts with Purchase Price

Important to many tax calculations is the adjusted *cost basis* for your home. This important figure starts with your purchase price—a figure known to the IRS as "original cost."

If you build the house, this is the price of the land, plus actual costs of building (architect's fees, building permits, contractor, labor, materials, utility hookups, legal fees). You cannot include the work you did yourself or unpaid labor by friends and relations.

If the home is a gift, you take over the donor's adjusted cost basis. If you inherit it, on the other hand, your cost basis will be the value at the time of the previous owner's death. Sell it soon afterwards for approximately that amount and you'll have no taxable capital gain.

☞ **Money-$aving Tip #43** *If you inherit real estate, you receive it with a "stepped-up" basis, eliminating capital gains tax on any previous increase in value.*

That's Just the Beginning

Once you have calculated original cost according to the rules listed above, you proceed to adjust your cost basis. The higher the cost basis, the smaller will be your capital gain some day when you sell.

You can add costs connected with your mortgage: appraisal, credit check, inspections, mortgage origination fees charged for services, if they are not prepayment of interest. You do *not* include points, which represent prepaid interest and get a much pleasanter tax treatment because they are immediately deductible. If you refinance your mortgage, some refinance expenses are also added.

You may also be able to include commissions, recording fees, title search, lawyer's fees, survey costs, transfer taxes.

(Many of these are traditionally paid by the seller; you can include only those you actually paid yourself.)

Add to your cost basis special tax assessments over the years for items like sidewalks or street lights; if you own a condo or cooperative, add special assessments to cover improvements like a new boiler or renovated lobby. If you own a cooperative, your basis may include your share of the building's overall mortgage that you took on as a debt when you bought.

Adjusted Basis

Now that you've come this far, it's time to adjust your cost further. You will add in, over the years, money you spend for permanent improvements.

You must reduce your cost basis, however, by any not-yet-taxed profit on a previous home and by any depreciation you claimed (or could have claimed) while the house was used for a home office or rented out.

The IRS allows homeowners to add the price of improvements to the cost basis for their property, to arrive at an important figure known as your *adjusted cost basis*. This amount will reduce eventual gain (profit) when the property is sold. Your file should contain every scrap of paper pertaining to improvements, items that you may not have considered important enough to include.

☞ **Money-$aving Tip #44** *Be sure to add the cost of improvements to your cost basis. Keep an accurate record over the years.*

Repairs Are Not Improvements

You probably think that when you replace the broken glass in the attic window and paint over the water stains on the living-room ceiling, you improve the property. The IRS, of course, takes a different view.

Repairs, redecorating and maintenance have no bearing on your tax liability. *Improvements* are replacements or additions that increase the property's value, add to its life or adapt it to new uses. Repairs, redecorating and maintenance simply preserve the condition of the property. Those expenditures are of no interest to the IRS and cannot be added to your cost basis.

Sometimes the distinction is clear. Patching the roof is a repair; shingling a whole new roof is an improvement. In other cases, however, only a fine line separates an improvement from a repair or maintenance. Repapering your bedroom is simply redecoration; wallpapering a new room addition, however, is an improvement.

Classified as Improvements

When an extensive remodeling program includes items normally classified as repairs, redecorating or maintenance, the entire job is treated as an improvement. Painting, normally classified as maintenance, may be taken as an improvement when it is part of a new addition, or when it is the finishing touch after kitchen or bath modernization.

Do-it-yourself projects must include only out-of-pocket cost of materials, rental equipment and, of course, payment for outside help. Bills for seemingly small items should be saved; they can add up to a considerable amount over the years.

Starting Your Improvement File

Besides your purchase price, your file for improvement costs should include many items that might surprise you: putting up a fence, seeding a whole new lawn, planting shrubs and trees, for example. The list on pages 163–164 can be a useful guide, but an accountant's advice may help with borderline items.

The closing statement you received when you bought your home sometimes yields information about additional improvement costs. If you paid, at the time of closing, any special tax assessments for items like sewers or sidewalks, those represent an outlay for improvements.

List of Improvements

The following items are improvements that can be added to the cost basis for your home. In each case, repair doesn't count.

Additions such as:

bath	Curtain rods
breezeway	Deck
closet	Dormer window (new)
deck	Driveway (new)
garage	Electric wiring (new,
porch	rearrangement,
Architect fees	replacement)
Attic fan	Enclosing a porch
Awnings	Fences
Barbecue pit	Finishing a basement
Basement waterproofing	Fireplace
Blinds	Floor supports (new)
Built-in appliances, such as	Floors (new)
dishwasher	Floor covering
garbage disposal unit	Garage door opener
microwave oven	Gas grill
stove	Heating units (new)
Built-in furniture	Hot tub
Cabinets (new or replaced)	Insulation
Ceiling fans	Intercom
Central air-conditioning	Kitchen fan
Chandeliers	Landscaping
Countertops	Lamp post

Locks
Mailboxes
Paneling
Patio
Pipes, drainage, sump pump
  (new or replacements)
Phone outlets
Plumbing fixtures
  replacing
  sink
  tub
  toilet
Pool
Repaving driveway
Replacing whole window unit
Roof (new or reshingled)
Satellite dish
Screens (new)

Security system
Septic tank
Sheds and outbuildings
Siding (new)
Skylight
Smoke alarms
Spotlights
Sprinkler system
Storm windows (new)
Swing set
Termite-proofing
Trees
Walls (moving,
  strengthening)
Wall-to-wall carpeting
Water heater
Waterproofing
Well

Repairs, Redecorating, Maintenance

The following items are not improvements and may *not* be added to your cost basis.

Fixing gutters
Mending leaks
Patching plaster
Patching roof
Repainting exterior
Repainting interior

Wallpapering
Repairing appliances
Replacing broken window
  panes
Resealing driveway

Yearly Income Tax Deductions

Those expenses that are yearly deductions against current income represent cash-back money in your pocket. They mean that Uncle Sam is paying part of your expenses, that your income tax bill will be lower or your refund higher than it would be otherwise.

Add up all your income tax deductions, including state income tax, investment income expense, charitable deductions, property taxes and real estate interest payments. Compare the figure with the standard deduction to see if it pays you to itemize.

Except for moving expenses, all the deductions listed in this chapter apply only if you itemize. In some instances, the taxpayer is better off taking a standard deduction. Most homeowners, however, find they come out ahead if they itemize. Where state income taxes are relatively high, or the taxpayer makes substantial charitable contributions or has significant medical expenses, itemizing is usually the better course.

Property Taxes

Property taxes on all real estate you own (not just your principal residence) are fully deductible against current income.

If your property taxes are paid by your lender from money placed in an escrow account, you deduct not the amounts sent with your monthly payment but rather the actual property tax paid. Your lender should forward receipted tax bills and should also render a yearly report of disbursements from your escrow account (save that also.) If you don't receive those papers, call or write and ask for them.

You may deduct the property tax paid directly on your individual condominium unit and also your proportionate share of property taxes paid on common elements. The condominium association provides documentation on this for the IRS. The owner of shares in a cooperative may deduct a percentage of property taxes paid by the corporation that owns the land and building.

☞ **Money-$aving Tip #45** *All property taxes you pay, even on a campsite or potential building lot, are income-tax deductible for the year in which you pay them.*

Mortgage Interest Payments

Mortgage interest is completely deductible for the year in which you pay it, with the following limitations:

You may deduct interest paid on mortgage loans totaling up to one million dollars used to buy, build or improve your principal residence plus a second home. The IRS calls such loans *acquisition debt.*

Besides the million-dollar acquisition debt, (which includes later home improvement), you may also deduct interest on up to $100,000 in further borrowing against your home, no matter what the proceeds are used for.

In addition to the items normally deductible, certain others are immediately deductible for the year in which you purchase or sell your home. Foremost among these are the "points" paid to a lending institution to enable you to get a mortgage loan. They represent payment for the use of money and are immediately deductible as interest.

☞ **Money-$aving Tip #46** *Points paid at closing are deductible whether paid by you or the seller.*

Only points paid on a loan for the purchase or improvement of your principal residence are immediately deductible. Points paid on a refinance mortgage, a loan to purchase a second home or a mortgage on income property must be spread over the life of the loan.

No matter how you and the seller adjusted property tax payments at closing, you are entitled to deduct the share of the year's taxes that cover your actual ownership, including the date of sale.

The Home Office

You may take a deduction for home office expenses if you use part of your home regularly and exclusively as *either:*

- your *principal place of business* for any trade or business, or
- a place to *meet or deal with patients, clients or customers* in the normal course of your business (Occasional meetings and telephone calls are not sufficient), or
- a *separate free-standing building* (a studio, for example) if it is used exclusively and regularly, even if it does not meet the first two requirements.

You need not meet all these criteria; any one of the three above will qualify the area for home-office deduction.

If you are an employee, the IRS says the office must be for the convenience of your employer and not just appropriate or helpful in your job. Employees seldom qualify for home-office deductions. (You may, of course, use a home office for some sideline business.)

Unless the area is used for a trade or business, you cannot deduct expenses for a home office, even if the activities performed there produce income.

Home Office Records To Keep

If your deduction is questioned, you should be prepared to prove the use of the area. If you receive clients and customers there, a log of visitors and an appointment book or diary of work done, kept regularly, will be valuable. Your separate business telephone line helps prove exclusive and regular use. The presence of business furniture and equipment lends substance to your claim. Photographs of your office can't hurt. A home office deduction often "red flags" an income tax return for audit. Take the deduction by all means if you are qualified but consult an accountant to check the rules.

How To Qualify

The IRS requires that certain criteria be met to qualify for a home business deduction.

Exclusive use. If you conduct business in a den that is sometimes used for playing bridge and your daughter's sleep-over parties, the area will not qualify.

Principal place of business. If you conduct your business at more than one location and claim your home office as your principal place of business, the IRS will zero in on the question: What portion of your income do you earn in the home office? Also relevant are the amount of time spent at each location and the facilities available at each.

Calculating the Home Business Deduction

You can calculate the percentage of your house expenses used for business by square footage or, if your rooms are about the same size, by the number of rooms used.

If your house contains 2,000 square feet and you use a 10 foot by 20 foot room as your office (200 square feet), you are using 10 percent of the building for your office. Your office area need not be a separate room, although a divider is helpful. If all the rooms in your five-room house are about the same size, and you use one as an office, you can claim one-fifth, or 20 percent, of the home's expenses for business.

You cannot deduct more than your net earnings from your home-centered business. You may deduct the entire cost of certain expenses incurred solely for your office area, most often painting and repairs. You may also deduct your proportionate share of expenses for the whole building.

Depreciation and the Home Office

The concept of depreciation allows you to write off as a so-called expense a portion of the cost of your home if used as a business. From your adjusted cost basis subtract the value of your lot (land does not depreciate). This gives you the cost basis for the building. Divide that by 31.5, because you are allowed to depreciate business property over a period of 31.5 years. The result is the amount of depreciation that could be claimed each year if the whole building were used for an office; you will multiply that by your home-office percentage to arrive at one year's deduction.

When you make major improvements to your building, they are added to your cost basis and the proper percentage of those improvements may also be depreciated.

How To Report

Your home office deduction will be calculated on Form 8829, which is usually attached to your return. The self-employed will claim a portion through the home-office deduction on schedule C, on which they report business income. The remainder will be taken as personal deductions on schedule A.

Once depreciation is involved, many do-it-yourselfers seek professional help with their tax returns; the self-employed may already be using an accountant for their business. If you claim a home office deduction, have an accountant calculate your business "expense" for depreciation on part of your building.

When You Sell

Use of part of your home for business purposes has tax consequences when you sell. All depreciation claimed over the years will be subtracted from your cost basis, resulting in a higher figure for capital gain. This may not matter if you are using the special homeowners' tax breaks explained earlier in this chapter.

If, however, you still have a home office in the year you sell, the homeowners' tax treatment will apply to only part of your profit; the portion attributable to your business use (that same percentage figured above) will be immediately taxable.

On the other hand, if you have a loss when you sell, you may not deduct any loss attributable to your own residence, but you may take a loss for the portion that represents business property—your ongoing home office.

Selling Costs

Whether or not you end up paying tax on profit for the sale of your house, it is necessary to calculate that profit (known to the IRS as your gain). And just as you adjusted your cost basis for the house, so will you adjust your sale price, subtracting from it certain costs of selling to arrive at the figure the IRS calls your amount "realized."

☞ **Money-$aving Tip #47** *Be sure to deduct costs of selling to arrive at your adjusted sale price.*

The largest of these will probably be advertising costs, if you sell the property yourself, or real estate commission if you sell through a real estate agent. You will also deduct legal fees, costs of proving title, and if you actually paid them, loan fees for your buyer, survey, appraisal, engineer's report, inspections and recording fees.

Computing Gain

Gain is, of course, the accountant's term for what you think of as your profit on the sale. Because it involves the sale of an asset, it is classified as a capital gain. If you are not using one of the special homesellers' tax breaks, your profit will be taxed at whatever capital gains rates apply at the time you sell. Your *capital gain* is your adjusted sale price minus your adjusted cost basis.

Total Amount Realized

For the year you sell, you will attach Form 2119, "Sale of Your Home," to your income tax return. If some time in the past you sold one or more principal residences and postponed the tax on the profit, the profit on this sale will also include the figure for postponed gain on a previous home or homes.

The IRS allows no deduction for losses on the sale of your own home. There's no way to use a current loss to advantage on your income tax return. It won't matter what sort of misfortune you may have run into.

Even if you have a nondeductible loss, be sure to report your home sale, so the IRS will have a matching return from you to go with the Form 1099 it will receive from the person conducting your closing.

Special Tax Treatments

You may eliminate paying federal income tax on all or part of that gain, temporarily or permanently, if you

- took back financing—held the buyer's mortgage.
- bought a replacement home within the past two years or plan to buy one in the next two years, or

- are aged 55 or older on the date of sale.

Installment Sale Treatment

When you sell real estate and receive payment in more than one year, you can elect installment sale treatment for your gain. (You can also pay the total tax due immediately, if you prefer. But once you start installment treatment, you must continue it.)

In the most common installment situation, you take back financing, acting as lender for your buyer by holding a mortgage. You will receive payment for the property month by month over a period of years (or sometimes, with one large final balloon payment).

Each payment you receive includes

- interest on the loan,
- a return of part of the capital you invested (cost basis), and
- part of your profit on the sale.

Even if a special homesellers' tax break means the principal you receive, the sale price, is not taxable, the *interest* it earns while it's lent to your buyer is subject to income tax.

Besides interest, the mortgage payments you receive contain principal payments that gradually whittle down the remaining debt. Each principal payment is composed of two parts: (1) *profit* and (2) a return of your investment (*cost basis*). Only the profit portion counts as a taxable gain.

With an installment sale you owe tax each year on all the interest received and on that fraction of the principal payments that represents profit.

Installment sales are reported on Form 6252. They can be combined with other tax treatments. If, for example, you chose to use the one-time over-55 tax exclusion on the sale, your profit would be tax-free as you collected it. You'd owe tax on only the interest. Or you might postpone tax on principal received, using the special rollover tax treatment.

Rolling Over Your Profit

The IRS offers two major tax breaks when you sell your own home, the one-time exclusion of profit and the rollover. The rollover provisions apply to sellers of any age and may, within limits, be used more than once.

Important: If you replace one principal residence with another within two years before or two years after, the rollover provisions must be used with your sale. That particular tax treatment is not optional.

Rolling over your profit means postponing tax on your gain, if you sell your main residence and buy another of equal or greater value to replace it. If the second home is of lesser value, part of your profit may still qualify for rollover. You do not eliminate tax on your profit, but rather postpone it until you sell the last home qualifying for this special treatment.

Both the original and the replacement residences must be your main home. None of the rollover provisions apply to a second home. Replacing a lakeside cottage you use on summer weekends with a ski chalet for winter months won't qualify.

If you change your own home to rental property, profit on its sale no longer qualifies for rollover. The IRS says, however, that it may be temporarily rented out as a convenience before sale without losing its primary residence status. Questions about how long that might apply could be taken to an accountant or tax lawyer.

If your new home is of greater value than your previous one, you postpone tax on all of your profit. When you report your sale on Form 2119, the adjusted sale price of the former home and the cost of the new one are compared. You need not put the actual dollars you receive for the old home into purchasing the new one. The IRS is not concerned about the amount of mortgage on either house. Only the adjusted sale price and replacement cost are relevant.

Any money spent on improvements during the four-year period counts toward the replacement cost of the new home. If, for example, you buy a replacement for $5,000 less than the adjusted sale price of your old home, spending $5,000 on improvements within the required period will qualify all your profit for rollover treatment.

New Home Costing Less

If your replacement home costs less than the adjusted sale price of your previous home, you must pay tax for the year of sale on part or all of your profit. For example, sell for $200,000 with $60,000 profit, buy a replacement for $180,000, and you'd pay tax on $20,000 of your gain ($200,000 minus $180,000). Tax on the remaining $40,000 is postponed.

The replacement residence must be owned within two years of the date of sale for the first one. The requirement could cover two years before the sale or as long as two years after. In some cases you might have bought your new home the year you sold the first one; it would still meet the within-two-years requirement, which actually covers a four-year period around the sale of your present residence.

The only extensions of time allowed are for members of the armed forces and people living outside the United States. The IRS states firmly that it makes no other exceptions, not even for circumstances beyond your control, as when, for example, the house you are building burns down before you can occupy it.

You may use only part of the property as a home: a farm, perhaps, or one apartment in a four-family house. In that case, the IRS considers that you have had two sales, one of your own home and one of income property. The profit is divided, and you can apply the special provisions only to that fraction that really represents your residence.

Reporting the Sale

IRS Form 2119 guides you through the steps involved in calculating taxable and postponed profit. If you intend to buy a replacement residence within the two-year period but have not yet done so when you file your tax return, you can choose one of two options:

1. You can pay tax on your profit now and, if and when you buy a house within the time limit, file an amended return for a refund of the tax paid plus interest.
2. Or you can state your intention to buy a replacement, not pay tax, and then amend your return, detailing the replacement home you do buy. If in the end you do not purchase a replacement, you would then owe the tax that would have been due, plus interest.

If you finance the sale and take back the buyer's mortgage, you can still use the rollover provisions to shield all or part of the principal payments you receive from tax. Installments and rollover treatments can be combined.

State Taxes May Differ

The regulations in this chapter apply to federal income tax. Many states use the same guidelines; yours might not. Check whether your state offers the same tax benefits.

A professional tax preparer is helpful for the year in which you sell your home.

Golden Benefits

Homeowners aged 55 or older selling a long-time main home may have no federal tax due, ever, on profit up to $125,000—and that $125,000 profit could include the postponed untaxed gain on a previous home or a whole string of homes.

This tax treatment uses some of the same rules that apply to the rollover provisions. The definition of a principal residence is the same. Gain is calculated in the same way.

The over-55 tax break *differs,* however, in that it is not mandatory. You choose when to use it. It can be used only once in your lifetime, and it eliminates entirely, rather than merely postponing, capital gains tax.

Ownership and Occupancy Requirements

The over-55 tax break differs also in that it does not always require the property to be your main home on the date of sale. The house must have been owned and occupied as your primary residence for at least three of the five years before you sell. For this tax break only, the IRS doesn't care what you did with the house during the other two years. You could even have moved out and converted it to rental property (but for less than two years).

The three-year period of occupancy may be continuous or interrupted. Short vacations or absences are considered periods of use even if the property is rented temporarily.

If you are in a nursing home, an exception is made to the time limits. You can satisfy the requirement if during the five years before the sale you spent at least one year in your home and at least two others in a state-licensed or city-licensed nursing home or similar facility.

Age Requirements

You must be 55 or older by the date the house is sold. It will not be enough that you turned 55 before the end of the tax year.

Jointly Owned Home

If you and your spouse own the home together, only one of you needs to meet the age, ownership and occupancy requirements. *If two unrelated persons own together,* each share is treated as that taxpayer's separate transaction. A brother and sister, each aged over 55, for example, could sell their home and each claim up to $125,000 tax-free profit on separate tax returns.

The Tainted Spouse

Most problems in applying the over-55 regulations center around the one-time use of the exclusion and the status of the spouses.

The exclusion is, of course, open to unmarried homesellers. But if you are married, both spouses must "join" in the decision to use it. And once that is done, neither can ever use it, or join in its use, again. This is true even for the spouse who may not have owned the home at all.

Two seniors who never used the exclusion and who are contemplating marriage, may intend to sell their old homes and buy one together. They should consider selling both before their wedding day. Even if they marry soon after and file a joint tax return for that year, each may take $125,000 tax-free profit, because *on the date of sale* neither seller was married to anyone who ever used the exclusion. Unless both homes are sold before the wedding, they can take only one exclusion between the two of them.

How the Agent Can Help

If you do not have an accountant or tax preparer, the broker will have names to suggest. If you are missing any documents connected with the purchase of your home, both the listing and particularly the selling broker may be able to furnish copies of many of them. Brokers are required to keep your file for a number of years; many agents keep them indefinitely.

Commonly Asked Questions

Q. *If I sell my main home and buy an RV to travel in, could the vehicle qualify as a replacement residence?*

A. It could if it is the place you actually live most of the time, and if it has cooking and sleeping facilities.

Q. *I am over 55 and sold my long-time home with a capital gain of about $75,000. If I use the one-time exclusion, can I still use the remaining $50,000 to exclude profit some time in the future on another home?*

A. You cannot. One-time means just that. Even if your profit is less than $125,000, claiming the exclusion will still use up the whole tax-free opportunity. There is no leftover exclusion, because you cannot use it a second time.

Q. *Is it enough if I turn 55 later in the calendar year I sell?*

A. To use the exclusion, you must be at least 55 on the day you close the transaction. You could offer the house for sale and even sign a contract before you reached 55, but you should not actually complete the sale until your 55th birthday.

```
┌─────────────────────────┐
│  ┌───────────────────┐  │
│  │  CHAPTER 14       │  │
│  └───────────────────┘  │
└─────────────────────────┘
```

Ownership Tips for Your New Castle

Know Your Home

Before you have even bought your home, when you are accompanying a home inspector, you have a chance to learn about the building's water and gas shutoffs and its fuse box. Inquire also about the shutoffs for individual plumbing fixtures, stoves, furnace and water heater.

After you move in, it can be helpful to attach bright rags or tags to the gas shutoff valve and the main water shutoff, so they can be found easily in an emergency. The location of various circuits should be marked next to your fuses or circuit breakers. Mark shutoffs for gas, water and electricity, and see that family members know where to find them. For appliances, keep manuals in a file, along with date purchased, serial numbers, model numbers and records of service calls.

Handy to one telephone should be a list of emergency phone numbers, not only 911 but your police and fire departments' own numbers, nearest ambulance and emergency rooms, the family's general practitioner, school offices and work phone numbers for adults.

Home Security

Burglars do not want to spend much time getting into your home, and anything you can do to make forced entry more difficult is in your favor.

Lights

Lighting your exterior and avoiding shrubbery that affords good hiding places is probably your first line of defense. Outside lights can be installed to go on automatically if anyone moves within a few yards. Others can be set on timers or photoelectric cells to go on at dusk and off at dawn.

Doors and Locks

Locks on your outside doors should include deadbolts. Also recommended are locks that require an inside key to be opened. When you are home, however, form the habit of keeping your keys in the locks, so you'd have no delay in getting out in case of a fire emergency.

Consider installing a peephole of the type used for hotel rooms, so that you can see your caller before unlocking your door. Sliding glass doors can be secured with bars or locking pins. Garage doors should always be kept closed and locked. This is particularly important with attached garages, which furnish a burglar with privacy for a leisurely entry into your home. Make sure the door from garage to the house is deadbolted.

Security Systems

Installation of a security system can be added to your cost basis for the house as a permanent improvement. Its effectiveness as a deterrent is demonstrated by the fact that you will qualify for a discount on your homeowners insurance.

The simplest systems simply sound an alarm when an intruder disturbs them. More complex and expensive installations will not only sound an alarm but also contact your police department. (False alarms will probably result in charges.)

Environmental Hazards

Testing for radon, soon after you move into your home, can be reassuring. Test kits can be bought at hardware stores, but if you are doing it yourself, it is essential to follow directions exactly. Should your home contain excess amounts of this carcinogenic gas, proper ventilation of your basement area is a fairly inexpensive solution to the problem.

Lead is particularly hazardous for small children, who can suffer brain damage if they ingest flecks of lead-based paint, which was extensively used before 1978. The process of scraping and removing lead paint releases extremely harmful dust into the air. It is best done by a qualified professional when children are not in residence. In some cases, peeling and flaking paint can be covered and sealed off.

Lead in drinking water can be minimized by letting the water run for a couple of minutes first thing in the morning when it has been standing in your pipes all night. Hot water leaches lead more quickly, so it's best to get in the habit of starting your cooking with cold water.

Energy Savings

In many areas, local utility companies or fuel oil suppliers offer free energy audits. If the service is available, consider calling for it soon after you move into your new home. A professional check for heat-loss areas can be valuable to you.

Insulation probably offers the best pay-back in fuel savings. Caulking and weather-stripping drafty areas makes a noticeable difference in comfort as well as fuel consumption. Common sources of heat leaks are fireplaces with faulty dampers; glass screens offer the best protection.

To cut water consumption, pay prompt attention to even the smallest drip or leak, which can add considerably to water costs. Replace faucet washers promptly, and solve toilet leaks. Experiment to see how many bricks you can place in your toilet tank without making the flush less efficient.

☞ **Money-$aving Tip #48** *Contact your local utility for information about saving energy, and inquire if any incentives are offered if you install more efficient light bulbs or appliances.*

You can expect considerable savings in fuel consumption if you set your water heater at the lowest possible point; this is also a wise precaution if there are small children in your home, to avoid accidental scalding.

Furnace and air-conditioning filters should be cleaned or replaced every few months in season. Setting your thermostat down on winter nights may help you sleep better as well as save fuel. Both heating and air-conditioning need not be set at optimum levels during hours when your home is not occupied. Consider installing a thermostat that allows you to preset various levels for each day of the week, to match your family's routines.

It is not always necessary to heat or cool the entire house. If one person works at home during the day, space heaters and fans may be enough for comfort. Unused bedrooms can be shut off during particularly hot or cold periods, with their heat vents closed.

Maintenance

Keeping your home in top shape will make resale some day much easier and more profitable. Attention to small details will add to the safety of your family and your enjoyment of the property.

On the exterior, make sure your doorbell and porch lights work and that the handrail is securely fastened. Clean your gutters of leaves at least once a year, and check downspouts by running a garden hose down them. Replace worn or loose roof shingles, fill and seal cracks in an asphalt driveway, check the flashing on your roof. Check your landscaping for driveway visibility and street entry. Screens on roof vents and a chimney cap will guard against birds or raccoons entering your property.

Inside your home, waterproof damp spots in your basement, test smoke alarms frequently and attend immediately to any cracked or broken windows.

Safety Precautions

Grab bars near toilet and bathtub should be fastened with long screws to studs in the wall; accidents can result if a wall soapdish or towel rack is used for support. Electric outlets and appliances in the bathroom must be located where they cannot be reached from tub or shower. An older home can easily be modernized with current arresters on bathroom outlets.

Stairways should be well lighted with switches at both top and bottom, at least one handrail firmly attached, with stair treads or carpet securely fastened.

Cleaning supplies, like medicines, must be stored out of reach of children. Toxic substances should never be decanted into food containers.

Remove doors from unused refrigerators or freezers, whether stored in a basement or placed outside for removal. Alternately, an unused appliance could be placed with its door snugly against the basement wall, so that children could not open it.

On sliding doors, particularly if they are of glass, place stickers at adult and child eye level to avoid accidents.

In the kitchen, store knives out of children's reach and always keep pot handles turned inward on the stove.

Hold periodic fire drills so your children will know how to react in an emergency. Discuss with children the need to leave the house immediately in case of fire and the various routes they could use to exit. Have a specific plan for exit from each bedroom.

Financial Aspects of Homeowning

If you move to a new state, inquire about any special property tax exemptions for senior citizens or veterans. These matters vary considerably from one state to another, and often you must make application for them.

In some states, but not all, special *homestead* rights can be claimed for a family's principal residence. In a few states, single persons may also have homestead rights. These rights may range from partial to full protection against the homestead's being seized by certain creditors. In some states, the rights apply automatically; in other areas, you must file an application.

Debts usually not covered by homestead protection include unpaid property taxes, purchase money mortgages, mechanic's liens, and in some states, unpaid alimony or child support. If your mortgage is foreclosed and does not bring enough at the sale to cover the debt against it, homestead in some states protects you against any judgment or claim for the shortfall. In at least one state (Texas), homestead laws prohibit any further borrowing against your principal residence after you have purchased it.

Refinancing Your Mortgage

When mortgage rates drop, you may want to pay off your present loan and place a new one. Because closing costs will usually be involved, you need to run some financial analysis to see whether the change will pay off.

An old rule of thumb said that refinancing was worth doing if you could drop your interest rate by 2 percent and expected to be in the house at least two more years. That advice doesn't take into account the widely varying closing costs involved in different refinance plans available today.

Find out what it would cost to refinance; in a few cases, you might pay a penalty for early payoff of your present loan as well as costs to place the new one. Once you know what your outlay would be and how much you'd save in monthly payments, it's a simple matter to figure how many months it will take to recoup your expense. If you remain in the house longer than that, the rest is profit.

☞ **Money-$aving Tip #49** *When interest rates fall, find out what refinancing your mortgage loan could save you and what it would cost.*

One danger: If you are already five years into a 30-year loan, be sure to compare your present monthly payments with those on a new 25-year loan. If you borrow the amount of your present debt for a new 30-year loan, your payments will be less, but you'll have ended up paying for 35 years. That might fit your objectives, but for comparison purposes, at least, find out what payments would be if the new mortgage were based on the number of years remaining on your present one.

☞ **Money-$aving Tip #50** *It's always worth contacting your present lender first to see if a streamlined procedure for recasting your present loan is available. If it is, closing costs, new appraisal and credit checks may be avoided or will at least be less expensive.*

Prepaying Your Mortgage

Whether it pays to send in extra principal payments on your mortgage depends on your interest rate, your disposable income and what you would otherwise do with the money. Income tax considerations shouldn't enter into the decision. Extra payments do mean a reduction in interest due and therefore a lower income tax deduction. But at the same time, if you didn't use the money to pay off your loan, it would be earning taxable income somewhere else. The income tax aspect is usually not worth considering.

If you want to pay off your mortgage earlier than scheduled, send in extra principal payments. Your savings on mortgage prepayments are easily figured. If you had a mortgage at 9 percent and you sent in one extra $5,000 payment clearly marked "to be applied entirely to the principal debt," you would owe $450 less in interest every year thereafter. Your monthly payments would remain the same, but with less interest due, more of each payment could be used to pay off principal. The debt would be cleared and your mortgage paid off months earlier than originally scheduled.

If you do want to cut the time remaining on your mortgage, it's just as effective to send extra principal payments once every month, once a year, or whenever you have a windfall. Be sure to check with your lending institution about the best way to identify the extra payments. If you're making an extra payment along with your regular monthly payment, send it on a separate check, clearly marked. And be sure to go over the annual statement you should receive each January to be sure the additional funds were properly credited to principal.

Biweekly Mortgages

Some mortgage plans involve biweekly mortgage payments, with half a monthly payment automatically deducted from your checking or savings account every two weeks. The results seem like magic to many borrowers, because they can't help thinking of it as "half a payment twice a month." But biweekly isn't twice a month at all. In some months, for example, you would make a payment on the 1st, the 15th and then the 29th.

Every two weeks adds up to 26 half-payments a year, the equivalent of 13 payments instead of 12 each year. It's that extra 13th payment that does the trick, cutting the length of a 30-year mortgage to 21 years or less.

Many lenders do not offer biweekly payment plans, but outside companies do, generally via direct mail offers. If you join up, usually for about a $400 fee, the company will automatically deduct half a month's payment from your bank account every two weeks and forward your regular payments on your existing mortgage monthly. Once a year, having collected that 13th payment, they send it to your lender with instructions that it be used completely as an extra reduction of your principal.

There's nothing to stop you from accomplishing the same thing on your own with a regular monthly mortgage. If you have the discipline, you can achieve the same results simply by making extra principal payments directly to your lender. One caution: Be sure to check your statements to make sure the additional money is being properly credited and is not just being stashed in your escrow account. If your mortgage company does not send monthly statements, it owes you at least a full year's review each January.

If You Are Facing Foreclosure

With many mortgages, a homeowner can technically be subject to loan foreclosure after even one late payment. But lending institutions are not eager to foreclose; most will work with a borrower who faces temporary problems.

Your first step, when trouble looms, should be to confer with your lender in person, if possible, or by phone (for starters) if your lender is an out-of-town institution. Your mortgage servicer is required by law to have a toll-free 800 phone number or to take collect calls. If you anticipate trouble making mortgage payments, contact your lender at the earliest possible moment.

If you have had a good payment record in the past, most lending institutions would prefer working something out rather than foreclosing and having your property back on their hands. Special departments are set up to deal with problems like yours.

Often, temporary payment schedules (interest only, FHA intervention for as long as a year) can be arranged to help deal with your one specific problem.

When you receive written notice that foreclosure is being instituted, the worst response is to ignore it and hope the problem disappears. Once the procedure gets too far along, considerable legal fees will have been incurred. Even if you could raise the money to pay the loan off and stop the process, you would be liable for extra costs.

Why not simply give up and wait to see what happens? Here are two very good reasons.

First, if the house is sold at a foreclosure auction, the proceeds may not cover the outstanding loan, accumulated back payments and the load of legal costs. In that case, the lender can sometimes seek a deficiency judgment against you personally. The judgment—money you still must pay—could cripple your attempts to get back on your feet.

Second, once you have gone through foreclosure, it becomes almost impossible to place a mortgage again. From a lender's point of view, foreclosure is much worse than bankruptcy in an individual's credit history.

If real estate values have plunged in your area, the best move is to ask the lender to take your house back and forgive the debt ("deed in lieu of foreclosure"). Your attorney can explore this matter for you. Occasionally, and if you can prove you are near destitute, a lender agrees to accept a "short sale," cancelling the debt in return for whatever the property brings on the open market.

But if your house can be sold for a sufficient sum to clear the mortgage, prompt action is essential. Get in touch with a real estate broker and list the house immediately, at rock-bottom price, for quick sale. If called in early enough, the broker or your lawyer might persuade the lender to hold the foreclosure process in abeyance for a few weeks. Many investors are out there looking for bargains in just such situations. You might be able to salvage your credit reputation, avoid extra legal fees and even realize leftover equity, if any.

Anyone facing foreclosure has special need for an attorney even though, in such a situation, additional fees are a burden.

How *the Agent Can Help*

If your state offers homestead protection against sei-
zure of your home for certain debts, a real estate agent
can give you information and, if required in your state,
tell you how to apply. The agent will also have data on
any special property tax exemptions you may qualify
for.

If you have trouble with mortgage payments and
selling seems the best solution, the agent can sometimes
negotiate with your lender to hold off foreclosure pending a sale.

Commonly Asked Questions

*Q. How much can we expect improvements to raise the
value of our home?*

A. Make improvements for your own use and satisfaction.
With the possible exception of careful kitchen and bath
remodeling, almost no improvement will be repaid in higher
eventual sale price. In some cases, for example, an inground
swimming pool can actually make a home harder to sell.

*Q. Is it a good idea to make extra payments on our
mortgage?*

A. There is no one right answer. The decision depends on
your particular financial situation. You shouldn't send off
your last penny to be tied up in your mortgage. On the other
hand, if money burns a hole in your pocket, using extra cash
to reduce your debt puts it beyond easy reach.

If you are an active investor, could you expect to earn more
with your extra money elsewhere? Putting it into your mort-

gage is the equivalent of making an investment that yields your mortgage rate, long-term, risk-free.

There's no one answer that's right for everyone.

CHAPTER 15

Investing in Real Estate for Profit

Real estate investment–buying property to resell or rent out–has been called not only the best way to build an estate but even the only way. Real estate investment, though, takes constant effort on your part.

You can buy shares of stock and then limit your effort to checking the quotations on CNN every night. Not so with a duplex three blocks from your home. You must be ready for a midnight call that a water heater has burst, and ready to buy a replacement promptly and arrange for someone to meet a plumber at the property that very day.

Real estate investment is not liquid. You can take your money out of the stock market with a simple phone call to your stockbroker. When your capital is in real estate, however, you shouldn't count on taking it out under, say, six months' notice. When employment levels get bad in your community, it's possible you can't get your money out until the economic cycle improves.

Getting Started

As an investor, you face some challenges—finding the right property, buying it right and then managing it. You also will need a lawyer who specializes in real estate, an accountant and a good real estate broker who is interested in helping you reach your goals. All three should be found before you make your first purchase. You'll need them to locate and then analyze the proposed investment. To prepare, talk with brokers, read the papers, visit open houses and develop some expertise so you'll recognize a bargain when you see it. Read everything you can find about real estate, but don't send hundreds of dollars for home study courses advertised on cable TV. The same material is available in local bookstores and for free in the public library. Take basic real estate courses at community colleges—the sort offered to beginning real estate salespersons. That'll give you the vocabulary and some basic information, and your fellow students may eventually prove helpful.

Start Small

It's wise to start small for your first few transactions, so you're not risking too much capital or taking on too much liability while you learn. A one-to-six-unit building in a familiar neighborhood near your own home is best. If the place needs fixing up, pay for a building engineer's inspection, so you'll know what you're getting into before your purchase offer becomes firm (the lawyer can help arrange that part). Try for property that will appeal to the largest number of responsible prospective tenants.

Forget about vacant land or building lots in resort areas. Land would have to appreciate markedly before it would pay off because it produces no income, ties up your money and requires tax payments. Judging which areas will be in demand in years to come takes skill and expertise, and even long-time investors can get burned. Land is no investment for beginners.

How Leverage Works

Traditionally, real estate investors have used leverage (other people's money) to pyramid a small amount of capital. If, for example, you had $100,000 and bought one piece of property that went up 5 percent in the next year, you'd make $5,000 in appreciation. To use leverage, you find ten such parcels, putting $10,000 down on each and placing ten $90,000 mortgages. If they went up 5 percent, you'd have appreciation totaling $50,000 in the same one year—and you'd control a million dollars' worth of real estate.

The traditional technique runs into problems, however, when local conditions change, employment drops, and it becomes difficult to find tenants who will pay enough to cover those ten mortgage payments. You may end up supporting the real estate by taking money out of your pocket each month—if you have enough money in your pocket.

Leverage techniques are among those touted by the TV gurus and taught in the mail-order courses. Much of that advice is outdated, however. For one thing, it is increasingly hard to find institutions willing to make loans to small investors with 10 percent down payments. At certain times, for small parcels of nonowner-occupied property, it's almost impossible to find lending institutions at all.

Finding Financing

For the type of small rentals (perhaps one-to-six-unit buildings) appropriate for a first investment, you may face some problem in obtaining financing. At various periods, institutional lenders have required large down payments from non-owner occupants.

One common solution is to seek seller financing. Unlike the sellers of single homes, small rental owners may not need their money immediately to buy other property. For their own income tax considerations, they may not even want full cash at closing. If your credit and income are satisfactory, it should be possible to find a seller willing to hold your mortgage, sometimes with a low down payment.

Analyzing Your First Investment

An accountant can help analyze any purchase before you make it. You use annual figures, calculating first the gross rental income. If present rentals are below market average, estimate the rentals you'd charge (just find out whether present figures are locked in with leases).

From the gross rental you subtract: an estimated allowance for vacancies and uncollected rents (in normal times, typically 5 percent of gross rental income); utilities paid by the landlord; heat (if furnished); property taxes; insurance; water charges (if paid by the landlord); trash removal; estimate for repairs (1 to 3 percent of purchase cost if in normal condition); janitor service, snow removal, lawn care and the like; and a reserve for future large improvements (new roof, furnace). An accountant can help estimate the proper reserve amount, a figure that might run, for example, another 2 percent of the value of the property.

With projected expenses subtracted from gross rental, you have the annual net operating income. From that, you then subtract debt service (mortgage payments). The resulting figure is your cash flow—actual dollars you can expect to take out of the property each year. If you have a minus figure, you have negative cash flow and had better think hard and long before taking on the investment. The beginner needs positive cash flow. It might be small, but the good news is that it does not represent your total return. Don't get into investment property if it doesn't yield at least a small cash flow.

To calculate your actual return, first figure your taxable income on the property. It should be less than cash flow, because of an artificial bookkeeping concept known as depreciation. You can charge, as a so-called expense, a portion of what you paid for the building (the lot is not depreciated). On residential property, divide the cost of the building by 27.5 to learn the amount you may charge each year for depreciation. (Commercial property is depreciated over 31.5 years.)

Subtract this depreciation amount from your net operating income to determine how much profit or loss you will declare on your federal income tax return. If it's a loss, discuss with an accountant whether you can take the loss against other sources of income. The rules are complex. If your total income is less than $100,000 and you actively manage the property, you may be able to claim up to $25,000 in losses against other types of income (salary, dividends, etc.).

With total income of up to $150,000, part of a loss may be deducted. Otherwise, your paper loss can be taken only against other passive income (the category into which all rental income now falls for tax purposes).

If you can take any loss on your income tax return, the next step is to figure the income tax savings that result, depending on your tax bracket. This figure is one component in calculating the true return from the proposed investment. True return consists of the cash flow plus the amount of principal paid down during the first year on the mortgage (amortization), plus estimated annual appreciation and income tax savings (if any).

The total annual return is then analyzed as a percentage of the cash you will invest. In order for the investment to fly, this return should be considerably higher than the return available on, for example, certificates of deposit. Otherwise, there's no point in risking your capital and making an additional investment of your time and effort.

The one-to-six-family residential buildings suitable for beginning investors will usually not support professional management and still show positive cash flow. In most cases, you'll have to manage the property yourself. It won't work if you have to pay someone else to change every faucet washer either. Save dollars by managing your first property yourself and by making your own small repairs.

How the Agent Can Help

Finding a good real estate broker is an excellent first step in building an investment portfolio. The broker who knows you are serious will educate you about being a landlord, help you locate suitable property, negotiate agreements with sellers, arrange inspections and help obtain financing. The agent will also work closely with your attorney and accountant; both of those professionals are a must for an investor.

Commonly Asked Questions

Q. What if I intend to live in one unit of the building?

A. If you do, obtaining financing becomes much easier. A VA mortgage is possible with little or nothing down on anything up to a four-family building. You can also obtain FHA and sometimes conventional financing, and maximum mortgage limits are higher. In addition, some or all of the projected rental income can be used to qualify for a mortgage loan.

Q. *Are those cable TV investors I see for real?*

A. They're probably not lying, but the successes they cite usually took place in earlier times and in other areas than yours. The testimonials about how "within six months of buying the course I owned $1 million worth of real estate" should really say "within six months I *owed on* $1 million worth of real estate."

It's not logical to think that you can buy property and immediately turn around and sell it for enough to pay your legal expenses and costs of owning it for however short a time, and still make a profit. Where will you find the buyers the original owner couldn't find?

Q. *What about the foreclosures described on cable TV?*

A. The TV programs don't tell you that you must usually buy for cash, that you can't inspect the interior of the properties, that most of the places listed in the newsletters they sell will be located in other states.

CHAPTER 16

Using Today's Technology for House-Hunting

Sometimes it seems as if the computer was invented specifically to handle information on the real estate market. Computers are naturals for managing constantly changing data—what's for sale, what just sold, what's the median price in a given neighborhood.

House-Hunting

Not too many years ago, you'd start your search in a broker's office by flipping mimeographed file cards full of information about various properties. You'd be warned that you couldn't really judge any house by that smudged black-and-white photo on the reverse side.

An energetic agent might make a special trip to the multiple listing office for the daily hot sheet—a list of properties recently listed by other firms.

You—or the agent—would make a list of addresses of properties that looked likely, and you'd handcopy or photocopy information from those cards.

And when you saw something that interested you, the broker would probably have to check by phone and often report that unfortunately an offer had been accepted on that particular property just two days before.

Today you can sit in a broker's office and see full-color photos of everything available in a multiple-listing system, and in the not-too-distant future you will see full-motion guided tours of the firm's own listings inside and out, including views of the neighborhood. If any property has just been multiple-listed anywhere in the system, full information is available to you immediately. As houses are sold, or sales fall apart, information on changing status is instantly entered into the system. In many offices, you will receive full-color computer printouts of houses that interest you.

Your needs and wishes can be entered into the broker's data base, so that when anything matching your requirements is listed, it's instantly flagged by the computer.

If you have Internet and World Wide Web connections at home, you can browse listings across the country, even internationally. You can get a feeling for the real estate market in any other area.

Whether you use a commercial server like America Online, CompuServe or Prodigy, or access the Internet through your college, place of work or a community server, it's easy to surf the World Wide Web for "business" listings. You can then narrow your search with the words "real estate." Thousands of individual brokers now post their listings on home pages, and you can limit your surfing further by geographic area.

You can also use "mortgage" as a keyword to find postings of current loan plans and interest rates offered by various lenders.

All of this preparation will enable you to work more effectively with an agent and eventually with a lending institution.

Either at home or through a broker's network, you can see street maps, property tax figures and other public information and census data for any particular area that interests you. Chambers of commerce offer guided tours; brokers post listings on their own home pages. Research of the real estate market has never been so easy.

And if you don't have computer capability, many agents use notebook or palmtop computers and even portable printers or modems to bring data right to your home.

Information on real estate listings surrounds today's buyer, on television, radio, Internet and Web, even in shopping center kiosks.

Office Equipment

For many years, secretaries struggled with carbon paper to type copies of purchase offers and contracts, and by the time the fourth copy was reached, none of the words came out in the proper spaces.

If your purchase offer went to a seller who was out of state on vacation, it would be presented over long-distance telephone, and the seller's acceptance might come by Western Union, with a confirming letter to follow. An offer subject to the approval of your attorney would go out by what computer buffs now call "snail-mail."

After you applied for a mortgage loan, the lending institution might wait weeks for your out-of-town credit report or for the return of verification forms from your employer.

Office equipment these days has streamlined the process out of all recognition. Listing information, research data, copies of contracts, all pour out of office copiers. Offers and counteroffers whiz from buyer to seller to attorney via fax lines and modems. Lending institutions lacking one last piece of information for your mortgage application will call for a fax from your stockbroker or banker.

Agents' Tools

In the old days, every broker's briefcase contained a small booklet of amortization tables, enabling the agent to calculate your monthly payment on any proposed mortgage. Today, hand calculators with built-in tables are programmed to judge your financial qualifications, estimate total mortgage payment and assist in appraisals.

The steel rule has been replaced by a radar-like gadget that measures room dimensions. Talking "for sale" signs broadcast property information to your car radio as you drive by. Instead of being switched to an answering service, your call may go to a pager and be answered almost immediately from a car phone.

And this is only the beginning!

How the Agent Can Help

More and more brokers can give you access to sophisticated programs to assist with your house-hunting. Many offices can guide you through the Web.

Meeting the appraiser or the termite inspector at the property is easier now that the agent carries a cellular phone—but the agent still has to arrange it. Calculating square footage is simpler with radar-beam gadgets and a hand calculator, but it still requires the broker's know-how.

As it has always been, finding the house you want to buy is just the tip of the iceberg. Bringing you into agreement with the seller, helping arrange your financial package, seeing the transaction through from beginning to end has always been the largest part of a broker's job.

Today's sophisticated tools enable the agent to give you better, prompter service. Buying a home, particularly your first, is an adventure and, with the right help, it can be an exciting, rewarding one.

Enjoy your new home!

GLOSSARY

abstract of title (abstract) History of a parcel of real estate, compiled from public records, listing transfers of ownership and claims against the property

acceleration clause Provision in a mortgage document stating that if a payment is missed or any other provision violated, the whole debt becomes immediately due and payable

acknowledgment Formal declaration before a public official that one has signed a document

acre land measure equal to 43,560 square feet

adjustable-rate mortgage (ARM) Loan whose interest rate is changed periodically to keep pace with current levels

adjusted basis Original cost of property plus any later improvements and minus a figure for depreciation claimed

adjusted sales price Sale price minus commissions, legal fees and other costs of selling

agent Person authorized to act on behalf of another in dealing with third parties

agreement of sale (purchase agreement, sales agreement, contract to purchase) Written contract detailing terms under which buyer agrees to buy and seller agrees to sell

alienation clause (due-on-sale, nonassumption) Provision in a mortgage document stating that the loan must be paid in full if ownership is transferred, sometimes contingent upon other occurrences

amortization Gradual payment of a debt through regular installments that cover both interest and principal

appraisal Estimate of value of real estate

appreciation Increase in value or worth of property

"as is." Present condition of property being transferred, with no guaranty or warranty provided by the seller

assessed valuation Value placed on property as a basis for levying property taxes; not identical with appraised or market value

assignment Transfer of a contract from one party to another

assumable mortgage Loan that may be passed to the next owner of the property

assumption Takeover of a loan by any qualified buyer (available for FHA and VA loans)

automatic renewal clause Provision that allows a listing contract to be renewed indefinitely unless canceled by the property owner

balloon loan Mortgage in which the remaining balance becomes fully due and payable at a predetermined time

balloon payment Final payment on a balloon loan

bill of sale Written document transferring personal property

binder Preliminary agreement of sale, usually accompanied by earnest money (term also used with property insurance)

bond Roughly the same as *promissory note,* a written promise to repay a loan, often with an accompanying mortgage that pledges real estate as security

broker Person licensed by the state to represent another for a fee in real estate transactions

building code Regulations of local government stipulating requirements and standards for building and construction

buydown The payment of additional points to a mortgage lender in return for a lower interest rate on the loan

buyer's broker Agent who takes the buyer as client, is obligated to put the buyer's interests above all others, and owes specific fiduciary duties to the buyer

buyers' market Situation in which the supply of homes for sale exceeds the demand

cap Limit (typically about 2 percent) by which an adjustable mortgage rate might be increased at any one time

capital gain Taxable profit on the sale of an appreciated asset

caveat emptor Let the buyer beware

ceiling Also known as a *lifetime cap,* limit beyond which an adjustable mortgage rate may never be raised

certificate of occupancy Document issued by a local governmental agency stating that the property meets the standards for occupancy

chattel Personal property

client The broker's principal, to whom fiduciary duties are owed

closing (settlement, escrow, passing papers) Conclusion of a real estate sale, at which time title is transferred and necessary funds change hands

closing costs One-time charges paid by the buyer and the seller on the day the property changes hands

closing statement Statement prepared for the buyer and the seller listing debits and credits, completed by the person in charge of the closing

cloud (on title) Outstanding claim or encumbrance that challenges the owner's clear title

commission Fee paid (usually by a seller) for a broker's services in securing a buyer for property; commonly a percentage of sale price

commitment (letter) Written promise to grant a mortgage loan

common elements Parts of a condominium development in which each owner holds an interest (swimming pool, etc.)

comparable Recently sold similar property, used to estimate the market value

comparative market analysis Method of valuing homes using the study of comparables, property that failed to sell and other property that currently on the market

conditional commitment Lender's promise to make a loan subject to the fulfillment of specified conditions

conditional offer Purchase offer in which the buyer proposes to purchase only after certain occurrences (sale of another home, securing of financing, etc.)

condominium Type of ownership involving individual ownership of dwelling units and common ownership of shared areas

consideration Anything of value given to induce another to enter into a contract

contingency Condition (inserted into the contract) which must be satisfied before the buyer purchases a house

contract Legally enforceable agreement to do (or not to do) a particular thing

contract for deed (land contract) Method of selling by which the buyer receives possession but the seller retains title

conventional mortgage Loan arranged between lender and borrower with no governmental guarantee or insurance

cost basis Accounting figure that includes original cost of property plus certain expenses to purchase, money spent on permanent improvements and other costs, minus any depreciation claimed on tax returns over the years

curtesy In some states, rights a widower obtains to a portion of his deceased wife's real property

customer Typically, the buyer, as opposed to the principal (seller)

days on market (DOM) Number of days between the time a house is put on the market and the date of a firm sale contract

deed Formal written document transferring title to real estate; a new deed is used for each transfer

deed of trust Document by which title to property is held by a neutral third party until a debt is paid; used instead of a mortgage in some states

deed restriction (restrictive covenant) Provision placed in a deed to control the use and occupancy of the property by future owners

default Failure to make mortgage payment

deferred maintenance Needed repairs that have been put off

deficiency judgment Personal claim against the debtor, when foreclosed property does not yield enough at sale to pay off loans against it

delivery Legal transfer of a deed to the new property owner, the moment at which transfer of title occurs

depreciation Decrease in value of property because of deterioration or obsolescence; sometimes, an artificial bookkeeping concept valuable as a tax shelter

direct endorsement Complete processing of an FHA mortgage application by an authorized local lender

documentary tax stamp Charge levied by state or local governments when real estate is transferred or mortgaged

dower In some states, the rights of a widow to a portion of her deceased husband's property

down payment Cash to be paid by the buyer at closing

DVA Department of Veterans Affairs. Formerly VA, Veterans Administration

earnest money Buyer's "good faith" deposit accompanying purchase offer

easement A permanent right to use another's property (telephone line, common driveway, footpath, etc.)

encroachment Unauthorized intrusion of a building or improvement onto another's land

encumbrance Claim against another's real estate (unpaid tax, mortgage, easement, etc.)

equity The money realized when property is sold and all the claims against it are paid; commonly, sale price minus present mortgage

escrow Funds given to a third party to be held pending some occurrence; may refer to earnest money, funds collected by a lender for the payment of taxes and insurance charges, funds withheld at closing to ensure uncompleted repairs or in some states the entire process of closing

exclusive agency Listing agreement under which only the listing office can sell the property and keep the commission except if the owner sells the house, in which case no commission is paid

exclusive right-to-sell Listing agreement under which the owner promises to pay a commission if the property is sold during the listing period by anyone, even the owner

fair market value See **market value**

fee simple (absolute) Highest possible degree of ownership of land

FHA Federal Housing Administration (HUD), which insures mortgages to protect the lending institution in case of default

FHA mortgage Loan made by a local lending institution and insured by the FHA, with the borrower paying the premium

fiduciary A person in a position of trust or responsibility with specific duties to act in the best interest of the client

first mortgage Mortgage holding priority over the claims of subsequent lenders against the same property

fixture Personal property that has become part of the real estate

foreclosure Legal procedure for enforcing payment of a debt by seizing and selling the mortgaged property

front foot Measurement of land along a street or waterfront—each front foot is one foot wide and extends to the depth of the lot

grantee The buyer, who receives a deed

grantor The seller, who gives a deed

guaranteed sale Promise by the listing broker that if the property cannot be sold by a specific date, the broker will buy it, usually at a sharply discounted price

hazard insurance insurance on a property against fire and similar risks

homeowner's policy Policy which puts many kinds of insurance together into one package

improvements Permanent additions that increase the value of a home

index Benchmark measure of current interest levels, used to calculate periodic changes in rates charged on adjustable rate mortgages

joint tenancy Ownership by two or more persons, each with an undivided ownership—if one dies, the property goes automatically to the survivor

junior mortgage A mortgage subordinate to another

land contract Type of layaway installment plan for buying a house; sought by a buyer who does not have enough down payment to qualify for a bank loan or to persuade the seller to turn over title

lien A claim against property for the payment of a debt; mechanic's lien, mortgage, unpaid taxes, judgments

lis pendens Notice that litigation is pending on property

listing agreement (listing) Written employment agreement between a property owner and a real estate broker, authorizing the broker to find a buyer

listing presentation Proposal submitted orally or in writing by a real estate agent who seeks to put a prospective seller's property on the market

loan servicing Handling paperwork of collecting loan payments, checking property tax and insurance coverage, handling delinquencies

lock-in Guarantee that the borrower will receive the rate in effect at the time of loan application

maintenance fees Payments made by the unit owner of a condominium to the homeowners' association for expenses incurred in the upkeep of the common areas

margin Percentage (typically about 2.5 percent) added to the *index* to calculate the mortgage rate

marketable title Title free of *liens, clouds* and *defects;* a title that will be freely accepted by a buyer

market value The most likely price a given property will bring if widely exposed on the market, assuming fully informed buyer and seller

mechanic's lien Claim placed against a property by unpaid workers or suppliers

meeting of the minds Agreement by a buyer and the seller on the provisions of a contract

mortgage A lien or claim against real property given as security for a loan; the homeowner "gives" the mortgage; the lender "takes" it

mortgagee The lender

mortgagor The borrower

multiple-listing service (MLS) Arrangement by which brokers work together on the sale of each other's listed homes, with shared commissions

negative amortization Arrangement under which the shortfall in a mortgage payment is added to the amount borrowed; gradual raising of a debt

net listing Arrangement under which the seller receives a specific sum from the sale price and the agent keeps the rest as sales commission (open to abuses, illegal in most states)

note See **bond**

PITI Abbreviation for principal, interest, taxes and insurance, often lumped together in a monthly mortgage payment

plat A map or chart of a lot, subdivision or community, showing boundary lines, buildings and easements

PMI Private mortgage insurance

point (discount point) One percent of a new mortgage being placed, paid in a one-time lump sum to the lender

portfolio loans Loans made by a bank that keeps its mortgages as assets in its own portfolio (also called *nonconforming loans*)

prepayment Payment of a mortgage loan before its due date

prepayment penalty Charge levied by the lender for paying off a mortgage before its maturity date

principal The party (typically the seller) who hires and pays an agent

procuring cause Actions by a broker that bring about the desired results

prorations Expenses that are fairly divided between the buyer and the seller at closing

purchase-money mortgage Mortgage for the purchase of real property, commonly a mortgage "taken back" by the seller

quitclaim deed Deed that completely transfers whatever ownership the grantor may have had, but makes no claim of ownership in the first place

real property Land and the improvements on it

Realtist Member of the National Association of Real Estate Brokers

REALTOR® Registered name for a member of the National Association of REALTORS®

REALTOR-ASSOCIATE® Salesperson associated with a broker who is a member of a Board of REALTORS®

redlining The practice of refusing to provide loans or insurance in a certain neighborhood

RESPA Real Estate Settlement Procedures Act, requiring advance disclosure to the borrower of information pertinent to the loan

restrictive covenant See **deed restriction**

reverse mortgage Arrangement under which an elderly homeowner, who does not need to meet income or credit requirements, can draw against the equity in the home with no immediate repayment

salesperson Holder of an entry-level license who is allowed to assist a broker who is legally responsible for the salesperson's activities (synonymous in some areas with *agent*)

seller's broker Agent who takes the seller as a client, is legally obligated to a set of fiduciary duties, and is required to put the seller's interests above all others'

sellers' market Situation in which the demand for homes exceeds the supply offered for sale

settlement See **closing**

specific performance Lawsuit requesting that a contract be exactly carried out, usually asking that the seller be ordered to convey the property as previously agreed

subagency Legal process by which the seller who lists property for sale with a broker takes on the broker's associates and cooperating firms in a multiple listing system as agents

survey Map made by a licensed surveyor who measures the land and charts its boundaries, improvements and relationship to the property surrounding it

time is of the essence Legal phrase in a contract, requiring punctual performance of all obligations

title Rights of ownership, control and possession of property

title insurance Policy protecting the insured against loss or damage due to defects in the title: The "owner's policy" protects the buyer, the "mortgagee's policy" protects the lender; paid with a one-time premium

title search Check of the public records, usually at the local courthouse, to make sure that no adverse claims affect the value of the title

INDEX

A–C

Acquisition debt, 166
Adjustable-rate mortgages, 45, 108–13, 118
Adjusted basis, 161–64
Adjusted percentage rate, 132
Adjusted sale price, 170
Adjustment period, 112–13
Agent(s)
  See also Law of Agency
  closing and, 145
  contract negotiation and, 97
  defined, 22
  determining home affordability with, 37
  developers/builders and, 63
  duty of notice, 25
  fiduciary duties of, 24–25
  financing and, 37, 53
  finding, 33–35, 37–40
  foreclosure problems and, 190
  homestead protection and, 190
  house-hunting and, 81
  loan approval and, 125, 134
  location considerations, 18
  mortgage loans and, 122
  moving assistance from, 154
  preliminary help from, 8–9
  referrals, 97
  relocation and, 37
Air conditioning, 182
Alimony, 128, 129
All-cash purchase, 100–101
All-risk insurance, 48
Amortization, 4, 111
Amount realized, 170
Annual payment adjustments, 48
Annual percentage rate, 107–8
Apartments, 5, 58–60
Application fee, 131
Appraisal, 133
Architects, 56–57

ARMs. *See* Adjustable-rate mortgages
Asbestos, 78
Assembling the exhibits, 132
Assessments, 61, 161
Assets, 127–28
Assumable mortgages, 115, 117–18, 139
Attorneys. *See* Legal assistance
Balloon mortgages, 120–21
Bankruptcy, 39, 130
Bargain hunting, 70–72
Bargain and sale deed, 138
Basements, 76
Basic (HO) insurance, 48–49
Bedrooms, 69
Biweekly mortgage, 187–88
Bonus income, 128
Brand-new houses, 51–52, 55–56, 57–58, 73, 93
Broker, defined, 22. *See also* Agent(s); Law of Agency
Building inspectors, 78–79
Buydown, 113
Buyer's agent, 23, 27–28. *See also* Law of Agency
Buyers' market, 2
Buyer's remorse, 131
Cancer, 77
Cap, 110
Capital gains, 4, 42, 171
Car loans, 129
Carpenter ants, 74
Cash, 52, 100–101, 138–39
Caulking, 182
Ceiling (lifetime cap), 110
Certificate of Entitlement, 8
Chambers of commerce, 203
Change of address cards, 147–48
Children, 64
Child support, 128, 129
Circuit breakers, 75
Closing, 39, 135–46
  costs, 52, 103, 132

Commission, 27, 128
Commitment, 132
Community mortgage plans, 130
Commuting time, 67
Comparables, 87–88
Computers. *See* Technology, and
    house-hunting
Condition of home, judging, 73–77
Condominiums, 5, 49, 50, 58, 60, 61,
    64, 161
Confidentiality, 25, 26
Construction, financing new, 121
Contingencies, 89–90
Contract for deed, 119
Contract negotiation, 85–98
Contractors, 57
Contract sale, 119
Conventional mortgages, 108
Convertibility, 111–12
Cooperatives, 5, 49, 58, 59–60, 161
Cost basis, 159, 160
Cost of Funds index, 110
Counteroffer, 95–96
Credit card debt, 42–43, 129, 133–34
Credit history report, 6, 8, 130
Credit unions, 105
Crime rates, 17, 73
Customer, legal protection of, 25–27

D–E

Deadbolt locks, 180
Debts, 42-44, 129-31, 184–85
Deduction, 3, 153, 165–70
Deed, 138, 146
Deed in lieu of foreclosure, 189
Deed of trust, 103
Defects, disclosure of, 26-27, 73
Deficiency judgment, 189
Department of Veterans Affairs. *See*
    VA mortgage
Depreciation, 169, 197
Developments (housing), 58
Disclosure, 23, 26–27
Discount brokers, 28–29
Dividend income, 129
Documentation, 141–44, 156–57
Doors, 180
Down payment, 7, 9, 54, 101, 126,
    127
Downspouts, 74, 183
Dream house, 9

Drinking water, 181
Dual agents, 31. *See also* Law of
    Agency
Duty of notice, 25
Earnest money deposit, 92–93, 98,
    127, 141
Education, and investment real
    estate, 194
Electric service, 75
Electromagnetic radiation, 77
Employment, 126, 128
Energy savings, 182–83
Engineer's inspection, 17
Environmental hazards, 77–78, 181
Equity, 4, 119
Escape clause, 90
Escrow account, 44, 47, 54, 140
Estate, 4
Estate sale, 71
Executor's deed, 138

F–H

Facilitators, 31. *See also* Law of
    Agency
Fair housing laws, 64, 95
Farmers Home Administration, 102,
    116
Federal Home Loan Mortgage
    Corporation, 104
Federal National Mortgage
    Association, 103-4
FHA loans, 114–15
    assumability of, 114, 117
    escrow accounts and, 47
    foreclosures, 82–83
    guidelines for, 130
    home defects and, 123
Fiduciary duties, of agent, 24–25
15-year mortgage, 113
Financing, 6, 39, 41-54, 195–96
Fire drills, 184
Five-year balloon mortgage, 120
Fixed-rate mortgage, 48
Flood insurance, 47, 50, 139
Foreclosures, 81–82, 188–89, 199
For sale by owner, 29–30
Foyer, 68
Furnaces, 182
Gain, computing, 171
Garage door, 180
Garage sale, 149

Gift, of down payment, 7, 126
Government National Mortgage
    Association, 104
Gutters, 74, 183
Hazard insurance, 48
Home, IRS definition of, 157–58
Home office, 167–70
Homeowners insurance, 48–49, 148
Homeowners' warranty, 74
Home security, 180–81
Homestead rights, 184
House-hunting, 67–83, 201–4
Housekeeping, 70
Housing developments, 58
Human rights considerations, 18

I–L

Improvements, 162–64, 190
Income, 43, 128–29, 134
Income tax, 3, 153, 164–65
Inflation, and real estate, 4
Inheritances, 42, 160
Inspectors, 78–79
Installment sale treatment, 172–73
Insulation, 76–77, 182
Insurance, 47–50
    moving, 150
    private mortgage, 52, 108
    settlements, 42
Interest/interest rates, 3, 41, 45–7
    adjustable-rate mortgages and,
        109
    mortgage interest payments,
        166–67
    refinancing and, 185
    teaser rates, 112
Internet, 202
Interview, for loan, 126–27
Investment real estate, 193–99
Job transfer, 37, 153
Joint tenancy with right of
    survivorship, 137
Judgments, 39, 130, 189
Kick-out, 90
Kitchen layout, 69
Land contracts, 119–20
Landlords, 126
Lawyers. *See* Legal assistance
Law of Agency, 21, 30
    agent's fiduciary duties, 24–25
    customer's rights, 25–27

hiring a broker, 27–29, 30
    seller's and buyer's agents
        compared, 23
    types of real estate licenses, 22–
        23
Layout considerations, 68–69
Lead hazards, 78, 181
Lease-options, 119–20
Legal assistance, 35–37, 38, 101
    contract negotiation and, 94–95
    lease contracts and, 119
Lenders, finding, 105–6
Leverage, 195
Liability insurance, 48
Lifestyle expectations, 13–19
Lifetime cap, 110
Loan approval, 125–34
Loan-to-value ratio, 108
Location decisions, 13, 72–73
Lock-in, 106
Locks, 180
Lot(s), 15, 56

M–O

Mail, 147–48
Maintenance, 53, 162, 183
Manufactured housing, 62–63
Marginal tax rate, 3
Military service, 128, 174. *See also*
    VA mortgage
Mobile homes, 62–65
Mortgage, 102–105
    See also Loan approval
    biweekly, 187–88
    brokers, 106
    choosing a plan, 45–47
    length of loan, 113–14
    PITI, 44–45
    preapproval, 7
    prepayment of, 186–87, 190–91
    refinancing, 185–86
Mortgage insurance premium, 114
Mortgage interest. *See* Interest/
    interest rates
Moving, 133, 147–54, 165
National Council of State Housing
    Agencies, 117
National Flood Insurance Program,
    139
Negative amortization, 111–12
Neighborhoods, and value, 72–73

Net worth, in equity, 4
New houses. *See* Brand-new houses
No-down-payment purchase, 101-2
Nonconforming loans, 105
Offer, 87, 96-97
Older homes, 74-75
$125,000 one-time tax exclusion, 4, 158-59, 176-77
Online services, 202-3
Open houses, 10, 79-80
Oral contracts, 98
Original cost, 160
Origination fee, 126
Overtime income, 128
Owners' cost, 88-89

P-R

Packing, 152
Parking, 61
Part-time income, 128
Peepholes, 180
Pension income, 128
Personal property, 91-92
PITI, 44-45
Plumbing, 75-76
Points, 27-28, 106-7, 126, 155, 159, 166
Portfolio loans, 104-5, 130
Possession, 140
Preapproval, of mortgage, 7, 100
Prepayment of mortgage, 113, 186-87, 190-91
Prequalifying, 100
Principal, 4. *See also* PITI
Private mortgage insurance, 52, 108
Profit rollover, 173-74
Property tax(es), 3, 45, 51-52, 59, 157, 165-66, 184
Prorations, 140
Qualifying, 41
Qualifying ratios, 43-44
Quit-claim deed, 138
Radon, 77, 181
REALTOR®, 22
REALTOR-ASSOCIATE®, 22
Recreational vehicle, 178
Redecorating, 162
Reduction certificate, 139
Refinancing, 185-86
Relocation, 37, 154. *See also* Moving
Renovations, 51

Rental income, 129
Renter's insurance, 50
Repairs, to property, 161-62
Replacement home, 174-75
Replacement value, 49-50
Resale value, 5-6, 8, 81
RESPA, 141, 142-44
Retirement, 128
Reverse mortgages, 4
Rollover, 158, 173-74
Roof, 74, 162
Rural areas, 102, 116-117
Rural Economic and Community Development Administration, 102

S-W

Safety precautions, 180, 183-84
School quality, 14, 17-18, 19
Seasonal income, 128
Secondary financing, 127
Secondary mortgage market, 103
Security, home, 180-81
Self-building, 57-58, 65
Self-employed borrowers, 3, 42, 126, 129
Self-movers, 149
Seller's agent, 23. *See also* Law of Agency
Sellers' market, 2
Selling a home, 169-70, 175
    closing costs paid by seller, 52
    points paid by seller, 27-28, 107
    seller financing, 118, 172, 196
    tax breaks available, 3-4, 158
    under pressure, 71
Senior citizens, 184
Septic system, 75
Sewers, 53, 75
Short sale, 189
Sidewalk snow plowing, 52
Sliding glass doors, 180, 184
Social Security, 128
Stairways, 184
State taxes, 155, 175
Steering, 18, 38
Storm windows/screens, 77
Student loans, 129
Subsidized payments, 116-17
Tax(es)
    adjusted basis, 161-64
    assessments, 161

breaks, 158–60
deduction benefits, 122
documentation, 156–57
gain, computing, 171
home offices and, 167–70
installment sale treatment, 172–73
IRS definition of "home," 157–58
mortgage interest, 166–67
new home costing less than old, 174–75
over-55 tax break, 176–77
PITI, 44–45
property, 3, 45, 51–52, 165–66
recordkeeping, 156–57
repairs, improvements, 161–64
reporting the sale, 175
rolling over profit, 173–74
selling costs and, 170
special tax treatments, 171–72
state, 155, 175
yearly deductions, 164–65
Tax shelter, 3–4
Teaser rates, 112
Technology, 201–5
Telephone service, 148
Tenancy by the entirety, 137
Tenancy in common, 137
Termites, 74
30-year mortgages, 112
3-2-1 buydown, 113
Title insurance policies, 136–37
Title search, 139
Townhouses, 49, 60–61

Tract housing, 16
Trailers. *See* Mobile homes
Transaction brokers, 31. *See also* Law of Agency
Transfer tax, 141
Trash collection, 52
Treasury index, 109–10
Trends, in homebuying, 1–2
Trust account, 44, 141
TRW, 6
203-b program, 114
203-k program, 114–15
Underpriced homes, 71–72
Unemployment insurance, 128
United Van Lines, 154
Unrelated persons buying together, 137–38
Utilities, 53, 148, 152
Vacant land, 157
VA mortgage, 8, 101, 115–18, 123, 130
   escrow accounts and, 47
   foreclosures, 82–83
Veterans exemptions, 184
Walk-through, 139
Warranty, 74
Warranty deed, 138
Water, lead hazards and, 181
Water charges, 53
Water heater, 76
Weather stripping, 182
Wells, 75
Wiring, 75

Over the past 25 years, the CENTURY 21® name has held the distinction of being the undisputed leader in the real estate industry. We have helped millions of people through the exciting adventure of selling their home or finding the home of their dreams. In the relocation process as well, CENTURY 21® experts have been with families every step of the way.

To meet the high expectations of today's demanding, value-conscious consumer, the CENTURY 21® System now offers an array of home-related products and services, including CENTURY 21® Home Improvements, computer online listings and homebuyer information services, *CENTURY 21® House & Home* magazine and other housing-related services.

As America enters the 21st century, the nation's most professional, best-trained home ownership experts are at your service at each and every one of the CENTURY 21® System's 6,000 independently owned offices in all 50 states and throughout the world.

Find This Book Useful for Your Real Estate Needs?

Discover *all* the bestselling CENTURY 21® Guides.

CENTURY 21® Guide to Buying Your Home

CENTURY 21® Guide to Choosing Your Mortgage

CENTURY 21® Guide to Inspecting Your Home